The Further Adventures of O'Neill in Holland

J. Irwin Brown

Alpha Editions

This edition published in 2022

ISBN : 9789356370012

Design and Setting By
Alpha Editions
www.alphaedis.com
Email - info@alphaedis.com

As per information held with us this book is in Public Domain.
This book is a reproduction of an important historical work. Alpha Editions uses the best technology to reproduce historical work in the same manner it was first published to preserve its original nature. Any marks or number seen are left intentionally to preserve its true form.

Contents

CHAPTER I. WHERE DID O'NEILL'S DUTCH COME FROM? ....- 1 -

CHAPTER II. SOME CHARACTERISTICS OF THE COMPENDIOUS GUIDE TO THE DUTCH LANGUAGE..- 3 -

CHAPTER III. HOW O'NEILL LEARNED TO PRONOUNCE. ....- 8 -

CHAPTER IV. AN INTERLUDE AND AN APPLICATION..- 11 -

CHAPTER V. THE 'COMPENDIOUS GUIDE' ON DUTCH SYNTAX. ....- 14 -

CHAPTER VI. THE GRAMMATICAL CARESS. ....- 18 -

CHAPTER VII. A GOSSIPY LETTER. ....- 21 -

CHAPTER VIII. THE SURPRISES OF THE MAAS. ....- 27 -

CHAPTER IX. THE THUNDERSTORM. ....- 33 -

CHAPTER X. THE DEVOTED NURSE............................- 40 -

CHAPTER XI. GOSSIP AND DIPLOMACY...- 44 -

CHAPTER XII. A STUDY IN CHARACTER. ....- 48 -

CHAPTER XIII. BELET! ....- 55 -

CHAPTER XIV. THE DAY-TRAIN. ....- 59 -

CHAPTER XV. SUPPER AT A BOERDERIJ. ....- 63 -

EPILOGUE. ....- 73 -

CHAPTER I.

WHERE DID O'NEILL'S DUTCH COME FROM?

We had all heard something of Jack O'Neill's adventures in Holland; and the members of our informal little club in Trinity College Dublin were positively thirsting for fresh details. There must be much more to tell, we felt sure: and we had a multitude of questions to ask.

Now the odd thing about O'Neill was that he didn't like to be interrogated; he preferred to tell his story straight through in his own way. He had evidently studied hard at the Dutch language, but without the least regard for system: and it was clear that he had been by no means careful in the choice of text books. Indeed, he seemed to be rather sensitive on this point, no doubt regretting that, in the ardour of his early enthusiasm, he had just taken the first grammar and exercise-book he could lay his hands upon, without consulting anybody. It was that curious plan of doing everything by himself that doubtless led him into the initial mistake, that of trying to get any sense out of "Boyton and Brandnetel".

A GREAT WORK.

Apparently he had kept that "literary find" by him for reference, and for digging stray idioms and rules out of, while he added more modern volumes to his working stock. This would account for his glibness in rattling off out-of-the-way phrases, and for that rich bizarre flavour which his simplest Dutch utterance undoubtedly had.

But we didn't know the worst.

Intentionally vague though he was in talking about his authorities, we ran him to earth (so to speak) at last in the matter of "Boyton and Brandnetel"; and had a happy evening.

That book was all O'Neill told us, and more. Printed on paper that seemed a cross between canvas and blot-sheet, it bore the date 1805. It was very Frenchified, and the English puzzled us extremely. Here is the Preface—or a part of it.

The following WORK was, originally, compiled by William Boyton. After passing f i v e E d i t i o n s , a Sixth appeared p a r t l y e n l a r g e d , a n d p a r t l y i m p r o v e d , by Jac.

Brandnetel. This last Edition was published, at the Hague, in the Year, 1751.

THE CIVILIZED LADY.

The several particles, of Speech, are arranged by the usual Order; and Declare with precision; every rule being followed, with practical exercise. This Mode, of teaching, being already a p p r e c i a t e d ; it will not be deemed Essential; nor do we, point out, the utility of it. As to Syntax; it is fully treated: whilst, l a s t   n o t   l e a s t , cares have been exercised, to unite ease with simplicity, accuracy with idiom, and animate the L e a r n e r . It aims at the pupil of H i g h - L i f e , and to acquire the Polish of the c i v i l i z e d   L a d y .

THE HAGUE, 1805.

This brilliant introduction raised our expectations to fever heat. We had never encountered such an army of commas before; and as for the English—!

A n y t h i n g , evidently, might be met with inside the covers of William Boyton's 'Work'.

BOYTON ANIMATES THE LEARNER.

The best of it, of course, was its extraordinary politeness. Every other question was prefixed with "Verschoon my", and went on something like this: "Zoudt gij zoo goed willen zijn mij toe te staan...". Then there were some plain and unornamental phrases such as "Men weet nooit hoe een koe eenen haas vangt".—This was labelled 'proverbial expression', and was translated, happily enough, by "The unexpected often occurs."

"Ik heb er het land aan je" was rendered mysteriously: "I have an objection", "I cannot agree".

That was puzzling enough, and delightfully vague! But for all that found the phrase doubly underlined by O'Neill and marked by him as 'useful for general conversation'.—

CHAPTER II.

SOME CHARACTERISTICS OF THE COMPENDIOUS GUIDE TO THE DUTCH LANGUAGE.

There was something good on every page, as might be expected from the very preface. And, withal, there was a steady process of boasting about its own merits that was most refreshing in the barren realm of grammar.

With mock modesty it dubbed itself on the title page, "The Compendious Guide," and followed this up with another title *"Korte Wegwijzer tot de nederduitsche taal."* The whole compilation was evidently the work of several generations of literary gentlemen, who aimed at the 'Polish of the Civilized Lady' in quite different ways, but whose united efforts certainly made 'The Work' remarkably incoherent.

> POLITE DIALOGUES.

We all quizzed O'Neill unmercifully about the Civilized Lady, and read some dialogues with immense satisfaction. So uproarious, indeed, did the fun become at last, that our neighbours on the stair came trooping in. Three of them were Cape-students, hard-working medicals, whom we never heard speaking Dutch, though we were well aware they must have known it. Like the others, they insisted on a full explanation of the tumult, and we showed them "Boyton". They didn't mind so much about the Civilized Lady; but when they turned to the Polite Dialogues at the end, a kind of shudder seemed to pass through them, as if they had got an electric shock—till finally they dropped the book and screamed with delight.

"Why! that's nothing so very odd", said O'Neill, looking hurt. "I have often used lots of those phrases." Picking up the dishevelled leaves from the floor, he ran his eye down a page or two and said: "Yes, of course. These things are all right: A bit stiff and bookish, perhaps; but correct, quite correct. You fellows needn't be so excited over nothing."

"Read us some!" clamoured the men from the Cape. "Read us some of the dialogues you imitated. Go on! Read!"

> HOW TO BUY A CASTOR.

"Oh!" said O'Neill, "almost any one of these conversations about common things is good enough. Here, for instance." And he took the book in his hand and walked about the room, giving us first the English—then the Dutch.

"TOUCHING BUYING AND SELLING.	**WEGENS KOOPEN EN VERKOOPEN.**
Have you any fine hats?	Hebt gij mooije hoeden?
This is one of the finest in the Country.	Daar is een van de fraaiste in 't land.
Yes, Sir; this is a dreadfully nice one.	Ja, hoedemaker; deze tenminste is ijsselijk mooi.
Just come close to the fire, Sir; and examine that hat narrowly.	Eilieve! kruip bij het vuur, mijnheer; en bezie dien hoed eens wel."

"That conversation," said the Professor, "must have been of immense help to you now in modern Holland?"

"Hm"—replied Jack doubtfully.

"O'Neill," said I; "Stop! You're making that out of your head. That stuff's never in any book."

NOT MURDERED?

"Well," was the hasty reply; "I see this isn't so good as some parts—not so practical, perhaps; but that's all here. Wait a bit.... Now listen. Here's something better. Hush!"

"BETWEEN TWO ENGLISH GENTLEMEN.	**TUSSCHEN TWEE ENGELSCHE HEEREN.**
My dear Friend, I am extremely happy to see you.	Waarde Vriend! ik ben ten uiterste verheugd u te zien (bezigtigen, of a house).
It has been reported for a certainty that you were taken by the Turks and murdered halfway between	Men heeft voor de waarheid verteld (als eene zekerheid verhaald) dat gij van de Turken genomen waart en gemoord halfwege tusschen

Leghorn and Civita Vecchia.	Livorno en Civita Vecchia.
But these atrocities did not befall me!	Maar deze gruwelen zijn mij niet gebeurd!
You are convinced it is not true?	Gij zijt overtuigd dat zulks onwaar is?
I am.	Gewisselijk.
I rejoice that you are restored.	Ik verheug mij dat gij heelemaal hersteld zijt geweest (of a building: geheel en al gerestaureerd geworden)."

GIJ ZIJT GERESTAUREERD.

There was a noise in the room at this, but O'Neill went on boldly to finish the Dialogue.

"Are you speaking in jest?	Gekt gij ermede?
I do not jest.	Ik gek er niet mede."

"That's enough—quite enough—for the present", said the Cape men. "We'll borrow the Wegwijzer from you, and bring it back safe.

"No, there's no fear we'll mislay it, or harm it. Much too valuable for that. But—you'll excuse us; we can hardly believe you've got that actually in print. And we're curious to know what kind of rules those learned grammarians give. You'll lend us this mine of wisdom for a few days, won't you? Thank you, so much.

THE ENGERT.

"And by the way, here are some of your own notes. What's this about *engert?*"

"Oh", said O'Neill; "that's a reminder about a neat phrase I picked up from my landlady. Did I never tell you?

"Well. When my cousin came over, you know, on his way to Germany, he stayed with me a couple of days. He's very athletic—a fine wiry, muscular young fellow, lithe as a willow, as you are aware. So I wasn't astonished at overhearing the landlady and a crony of hers discussing him. They used a rumble of unintelligible words about Terence, as he passed the two of them on the stairs with the slightest of nods, and mounted three steps at a time, whistling as he went. There was no mistake about their referring to him; and amid the chaos of sounds I caught the words *eng* and *engert*.

Curious to know how Terence's agility, or perhaps his swarthy complexion, had affected them, I turned up these terms of admiration in my dictionary; and found *eng*, 'thin', 'narrow'. The longer word wasn't there. But on the whole it seemed safe to conclude from *eng* meaning 'narrow', that *engert* would work out something like "fine strapping fellow and in excellent training". If that was it, my landlady had hit the nail on the head. For Terence had just been carrying all before him at the last Trinity sports.

Her admiring criticism I duly entered in my notes and kept for use.

Some days after Terence had left, the landlady was praising her son's cleverness to me; and to please her I just said that he was a wonderful boy. 'Mirakel van een jongen' was the expression I employed; and I was quite proud of it. But she didn't seem appreciative of my effort, so I fell back on her own idiom. Fortunately the lad was quite slender, and I could dwell with satisfaction on the suitability of my new word.

"Hij is zoo eng", I said. "Ja juffrouw hij is een engert!—een echte engert!!"

She received my encomium on her boy with speechless indignation, and rose and left the room. You can't be too careful", added O'Neill thoughtfully.

BETAALD ZETTEN.

"Jack," said one of the students. "I prefer your own notes even to Boyton. Haven't you some more? Ah, what's this?" he enquired, turning to some pencillings inside the back. "*Dat zou je wel willen*", he read aloud, "'signification doubtful!'

"And here's one marked '*commercial*': 'We'll consider the transaction as settled': Dutch apparently something like, '*Dat zal ik u betaald zetten*'. Here's another labelled, '*not deftig, but very popular*': '*Ben je niet goed snik?*' Translation *seems* to be: 'you're not quite able to follow my meaning.'

"Ah! No more? That's a pity."

"Oh I have plenty more," interposed O'Neill; "but not here. And you want to read this Boyton volume."

GEKT GIJ ER MEDE?

"Let me finish the 'Dialogue between English gentlemen', and you may have The Work.

The first Englishman says: "Ik bid U, mijnheer; laat mij geene onheusheid begaan."

Then the other, the man who had been so disappointed that his friend wasn't murdered, answers politely: "Ik weet zeer wel welke **e e r b i e d** ik U schuldig ben."

Up to this moment the two acquaintances seemed to have got on fairly well together in spite of some difficulties. Why two Englishmen when they met in Paris about the year of grace 1805 should plunge into a complimentary dialogue in Dutch, is not very clear. But that there was a lurking feeling of antagonism in the **g o s s i p ' s** mind towards his compatriot, seems to be shown by the remark that he now makes to wind up the dialogue.

DUIZENDMAAL VERSCHOONING, MEJUFFROUW!

"*Mejuffrouw* (!) *ik bid U duizendmaal om verschooning, indien ik heden eenige onheusheid omtrent U bega.*"

That was final. The returned traveller hasn't a word for himself, after he is called 'mejuffrouw.'

"Mind you, gentlemen," continued O'Neill, holding Boyton aloft like a trophy, "if I **d i d** try to stop too prolonged conversations in that gracefully irrelevant fashion, I had caught the trick of it from Brandnetel himself. You have only to go on heaping civilities on your wearisome talker's head, but take care to call him, just once, Mejuffrouw, and he'll have to go. It's a neat way of saying Good-bye. I never found the method to fail.

Some day I'll tell you how supremely effective I found that unexpected little turn.

Why it's nearly as good as *Zanik nouw niet*."

CHAPTER III.

HOW O'NEILL LEARNED TO PRONOUNCE.

"I never could quite understand," said Bart van Dam, the big Cape giant, who had carried off Boyton the week before, "how O'Neill managed, out of such an extraordinary book, to pick up anything of the pronunciation. For, as a matter of fact, he **d o e s** get quite close to some of the sounds; and I can nearly always guess what he is trying to say.

"When he is talking about that interesting Rotterdam street, the Boompjes, he doesn't make the first part rhyme with the English word loom, and then add **c h e e s e**, a thing I have heard Britishers do who should have known better. And actually, I have noticed he can distinguish **g o e d , g r o o t , g o o t**. That's promising.

> THE GOAT THAT RAN ROUND THE ROOF.

"Some of my British friends at the Cape, even after I graduated on English Literature and History, used kindly to drop Dutch words into their conversation, either to make it easy for me, or to keep up my spirits, so to speak. Oh never a talk of over five minutes, but little familiar terms like **t a a l , z o l d e r , m a a r**, and so on, would begin to be showered in, here and there. One of these linguists had taken me into his own back garden, (he was very fond of animals of all kinds and we had gone out to inspect those he had) when he began to explain the new improvements on his premises.

We got into a deep discussion on the right way of draining a flat roof. "Come here", said he, at last. "Look up there, and you'll see a **g o a t   o f   m i n e** running all round the open space!"

"Goat!" I exclaimed; "it'll fall!"

"Nonsense", he said, "not unless lightning strikes it. Firm as a rock! Now, isn't that the right sort of **g o a t   t o   c a r r y   t h e   w a t e r   o f f** ?"

He thought he had said goot in Dutch!

Well now, Jack's beyond **t h a t**. Who had been coaching him?

> A HAS A BROAD SOUND.

Naturally I turned up Boyton on pronunciation the very first thing at home—and the mystery was solved! I was amazed. Boyton excels in teaching the sounds. Here is an extract or two from his

REMARKS ON THE DUTCH PRONUNCIATION.

A	has a **b r o a d e r s o u n d** than in English, bal.
A A	has a **b r o a d e r s o u n d**, aal.
A A U	**s o u n d s b r o a d**, as in graauwen, to snarl.
E U	is described as resembling eu in Europe. For the **f a l s i t y** thereof, let the word be pronounced by a Native, and the **M i s t a k e** will be **f e l t**.
G	is a guttural letter difficult to an Englishman; it can only be acquired by hearing it from a **C i v i l i z e d N a t i v e**, e.g. gierig and gijzelen.
U U	No Englishman can emit this sound. It may be well heard in vuur (fire) and in guur. Consult a Dutch Instructor.
E I	This sound is beyond the powers of the unassisted English Organs of Speech. It must first be heard from an educated Hollander.
U I	It is **i m p r o p e r** to make this identical with oy as in boy; the native pronunciation must be followed.

There you have some of the Rules! They won't lead you far wrong, in any case. Then, to crown all, for fear the diligent reader wouldn't have caught the point yet, Boyton goes back to his favourite "Doctrine of the Native." Here it is:

The Editor places the learner on his guard against receiving wrong references, and directs him to an Instructor, or Native, whose Dialect it is, for the sound peculiar to each letter.

NATIVES.

Bravo, Boyton!

Three kinds of Natives he recommends the beginner to consult. He has them arranged in a sort of ascending scale—**the Civilized, the Intelligent and the Polite**.

The two former classes will help you with the pronunciation, or with Het.

From the latter you get idioms.

CHAPTER IV.

AN INTERLUDE AND AN APPLICATION.

"So our friend Jack had to ask always for the sounds of the words. That would be right good for him," said Bart, "and should have made his talk intelligible."

"Well of course it did," said O'Neill. "They always understood the **w o r d s** I used. It was the applications I made that hampered them.

"I had great trouble with a chatty old gentleman in the tram one morning going down to Scheveningen. It was just seven—I was hurrying to get an early dip, and he seemed bent on the same errand.

Attracted by my blazer and towel he opened conversation about sea-bathing, and then proceeded to discourse on the beauties of the landscape. He seemed chilled by the poverty of my adjectives, though I worked them vigorously.

A LOFTY CANOPY OF GREEN.

"Deze weg vin je zeker wel mooi?" he said at last, looking up at the arched green overhead. "Of houd U niet van de natuur?"

"Ja, zeker wel!" I hastened to assure him. "Ik houd er erg van—Het is prachtig! Net een tunnel van geboomte—van loofgroen."

Then observing the pleasure my encomiums gave him, I ventured on something a little more lofty and poetic. My landlady had occasionally talked about a "canopy," which, so far as I had understood her, I took to mean the vast cupola of hangings over the old-fashioned bed in my lodging. She used to say that the canopy was new and beautiful, and needed constant dusting.

I had always agreed to this, but never dreamt of hunting up a word that to all intents and purposes seemed the same as in English.

"Indrukwekkend schoon," I added. "Wij zitten, als het ware, onder een canopey (that was my landlady's pronunciation) van bladeren."

"Een kanapé, mijnheer?"

"Ja," said I, "een verheven canopy, niet waar?

Wij zeilen onder een groene canopy—verbazend—magnifique!"

BENT U EEN DICHTER?

"Hoe bedoelt U dat?" said the old gentleman more and more puzzled, and determined to find out my meaning.

"Wij zitten hier, niet waar?" I began slowly; then pointing to the roof of green over our heads, I explained: "dat alles vormt een prachtige canopy boven ons heen. Zeker wel?"

"Ik geloof het niet", said the chatty old gentleman. "De tram gelijkt ook niet op een kanapé; of meent U dat?"

"De tram niet," I exclaimed, "maar de boomen; kijk; het gebladerte, het geboomte en de hooge dak dat ze maken—dat alles zoo schitterend groen, dat is, mijns bedunkens, niets dan een canopy, uitgehangen zoo te spreken, over ons heen, in uitgestrekte schoonheid."

The old gentleman surely was a little dull. He said, "Ik begrijp niet goed wat u zegt. Waar is de canapé? Of bedoelt U soms een badstoel—op het strand?"

"Nee", I answered with a deprecating smile; "Ik sprak maar poetisch. **V e r h e v e n** ", I added with a wave of my towel towards the greenery overhead.

"Hé," said he with friendly interest, "bent U een dichter? Ik had U voor een schilder gehouden," he explained with a glance at my blazer.

THE CLOTURE.

"Ik—een dichter!" I returned modestly. "Neen; niet erg. Op een kleine schaal, misschien." **O n a s m a l l s c a l e** , I meant to say; but I must have mangled the **s c h** badly, for he didn't catch the point, and I heard him mutter: "Een sjaal! een sjaal, EN een kanapé!!"

"Ja zeker, mijnheer," I reasoned; "U ziet het zelf voor U—daar onder de boomen—dat IS hier een canopy—"

"Pardon", he interrupted, "dat is niet waar. Dat zijn gewone houten banken," he persisted argumentatively. "En wat bedoelt U met een sjaal?"

How pertinacious the old gentleman was! He stuck to me like a leech. I couldn't shake him off; and we were still far off the Kurhaus.

It was clearly a case for Boyton's conversational method.

AN INTERLUDE AND AN APPLICATION.

"Mejuffrouw!" I said firmly, leaning towards him, "Ik ken Uwe edelmoedigheid genoeg. Maar"—and here I added two nice little local idioms from the rich stores of my memory—"maar—U komt pas te kijken."

That told him he wasn't looking at the matter in true philosophic perspective.

But this I followed up, in a more authoritative way, with the assurance that I didn't at all agree with him. "Waarempeltjes," I whispered with elaborate distinctness, "ik heb het land aan je!"

The chatty old gentleman got off at the next h a l t e .

CHAPTER V.

THE 'COMPENDIOUS GUIDE' ON DUTCH SYNTAX.

Boyton's monograph on pronunciation is his finest piece of work. He never quite reaches that level elsewhere; and, if he is destined after a hundred and fifty years to achieve a name, it had better rest on his 'Doctrine of the Native' than on his Syntax.

So van Dam assured us, when our little party met in his room the week before Christmas.

We had all been busy; but busy or not, the Cape men found time to skim over Boyton's entertaining paragraphs, as, indeed, we guessed, from the frequent guffaws and readings that reached us from time to time through the closed doors. To night we had accepted an invitation to supper, before the holidays; and we were to hear his views on O'Neill's 'Guide, Philosopher and Friend', Boyton,—in other words the *Wegwijzer tot de nederduitsche taal*. Long since Jack had, indeed, got other and more modern manuals of Dutch, so that he was supposed to look now with a certain contempt on his former monitor: but the "compendious guide" had laid the basis of his erudition, and he had still a sneaking regard for its honest old pages.

NO DEFINITE RULES.

What we wanted, indeed, was stories from Jack himself: but we had exhausted the more dramatic of these; and to get the fine aroma of the others—there were still many others—we thought some acquaintance with the compendium's syntax was essential.

Van Dam had undertaken to put us up to any niceties he had been struck with.

The first thing he told us was that Boyton had no clear ideas of any sort, and never laid down any definite rule. This lent him a certain diffidence in regard to most points,—a diffidence which in the case of HET became positive fright. At the first mention of d e , h e t , and an **a d j e c t i v e** , he gives as much encouragement as he can.

ALL NOUNS TO WHICH HET IS PREFIXED ARE NEUTER.

It is not much.

An insurmountable Difficulty for the Englischman is the right use of the Particles, especially h e t . Sufficient rules cannot be given, E. g. het mooie kind: eene sterke vrouw, een zwart schip.

T h i s   i s   c e r t a i n ,   t h a t   a l l   N o u n s ,   t o w h i c h   t h e   P a r t i c l e s ,   h e t ,   d a t ,   o r   d i t , a r e   a d d e d   a r e   o f   t h e   N e u t e r   G e n d e r ;   o n t h i s   a c c o u n t ,   t h e   e   f i n a l ,   i n   t h e A d j e c t i v e s ,   w h e n   j o i n e d   w i t h   s u c h w o r d s ,   i s ,   g e n e r a l l y ,   r e j e c t e d .

Even this rule admits of an exception. E. G. It is never said: e e n s n e l   v o g e l :   d e   g r o o t e   p a a r d . But it is correct to say, if the meaning admits it, e e n   g r o o t e   m a n . (also g r o o t .) A native may be consulted with advantage.

When Boyton is labouring under strong emotion, the effect is always to increase the number of commas, colons, and other stops.

His agitation may also be traced in the way he harks back to any fundamental rule that he has already discussed ad nauseam.

DEN IS NOT A PURE NOMINATIVE.

It is quite pathetic to note how he urges on his readers to reserve their dezen and dien and den for the accusative.

It is good Dutch to say: ik zag dien braven man gisteren, *I saw that honest man yesterday;* b u t   i t   i s   v e r y   b a d   D u t c h , — w h a t e v e r   c u s t o m   m a y   h a v e   i n t r o d u c e d i n   s o m e   p l a c e s ;   t o   s a y —dien braven man heeft het gezegd.

Take some gems at random.

N.B. Prepositions are that part of speech, which are so called because they are, commonly, put before the words, which are subsequent to them, as o n d e r and o n d a n k s .

N.B. Most Adverbs may be distinguished from adjectives by this rule: If a substantive is added after them, they will make n o n s e n s e ; whereas, being joined to an Adjective or a Verb, they will make good sense.

"What I admire most," said van Dam handing back The Work to O'Neill, "is the elasticity of the rules. He says, for instance, that you can render I

know by **i k   w e e t** , and on the whole he is inclined to recommend that way of it. But he never commits himself.

"**It must be also admitted that there are other authors of good standing who employ the Subjunctive form where we might expect the Indicative and who say** IK WETE, **I   know** ."

IK GRAUW, IK KEF, EN IK KWEEL.

That's one of his rules!

As a matter of fact there is no finality about anything in these pages. O'Neill, you were in training for a poet when you took up this book. I confess I should have liked to hear you going over your fifteen classes of irregular verbs, on the model (say) of ik grauw, ik kef en ik kweel, or even of ik krijsch, ik piep en ik lieg.

There is a rich profusion of tenses too in Boyton. He needn't have apologized for being too simple when he furnishes you with four ordinary optatives and four future optatives."

A BOYTON TO THE RESCUE.

"You may jest as you like about Boyton", interrupted Jack; "but I tell you it's a book that has points. Do you know it once helped me to save a lady's life?"

"Save a lady's life!" said the Professor and the Philosopher in one breath. "We'll withdraw all we've said, if you'll prove to us, now, that the 'Compendious Guide' was ever the least good to any human being."

"Tell your adventure in your own way, O'Neill," a boyish voice chimed in; "and shame the cynics."

We all glared at the First-year's man—who was making himself very much at home for a lad of his tender years—but as he had nothing more to say, we let him off with a look, and turned to the lethargic story-teller.

CHAPTER VI.

THE GRAMMATICAL CARESS.

"You saved life with that Boyton-Grammar of yours, if I catch the drift of your last remark?" interposed the Professor magniloquently, as if he were addressing a public meeting.

"May I hazard the guess that Boyton on that occasion was rather a weapon of offence than of defence?"

"Well, you're right," said O'Neill. "Offence is more in Boyton's line. And he certainly did press heavily, that day, on a butcher's boy. You remember those slagersjongens that saunter about, in white linen coats, with great protruding baskets on their shoulders. They jostle and push wherever they have a chance, and whirl round with their cargoes of meat, so as to make you start. You know the tribe. Well, Boyton proved an admirable corrective to the insolence of one of these imps.

A HAPPY CROWD.

It was a day there was a sort of festival in the Hague.

From early in the afternoon there was a crush everywhere. The singels and the main roads through the Wood were filled with holiday-makers. Soldiers were parading here and there. Everyone was in the best of good humour; music in the distance rose and fell on the air; flags fluttered from the windows. Look where you might, there were bright dresses, prancing horses, snorting motors, and pedestrians of all descriptions.

I was one of the pedestrians.

I had been at my grammar in the morning; and after a long spell in the house had stepped over to Enderby's, and coaxed that lazy fellow out for a stroll. It was perfect weather, and the crowds were wonderfully well-behaved. We enjoyed ourselves finely 'under the green-wood tree,' till we were brought to a stand-still in a dense mass of humanity that was packed along the edge of a canal, scarcely moving. A procession or something had impeded the traffic some moments.

INNOCENCE IN DANGER.

There was a knot of butchers' boys right in front of us. They were roughly shoving their neighbours about, and seeing what mischief they could do. Horse play, in fact. They didn't seem to fit into Boyton's categories, either of 'Natives intelligent' or 'polite'.

Presently one brawny scoundrel began to throw stones at the occupants of a carriage that was slowly passing by.

I couldn't believe my eyes!

There sat an old lady of eighty or ninety, with soft white hair—the very picture of fragility; opposite her was a nurse in dark uniform, in charge of three dainty little children in pink and white—mere babies of three or four—with innocent blue eyes gazing all round them. And, actually, that ruffianly k n e c h t was about to bombard the group with whatever he had in his hand!

Bang went a big mass of something—presumably hard, from the rattle it made—against the side of the carriage.

Happily he was a poor marksman, that rascally slager; for at that short range he ought to have been able to demolish so fragile an old lady at the first shot, or at the very least have put out one eye.

As it was, he only knocked off her bonnet.

Enraged, apparently, at his poor practice at a practically stationary target so close at hand, he picked up another half-brick and wheeled, to take more deliberate aim.

The delicate old lady grew pale, and spasmodically fumbled with her parasol to shield the children.

NEMESIS.

I thought her eye caught mine; and, seeing there was no escape for her unless I interposed—no one till now seemed to have noticed the occurrence—I shouted, "S t o p ,   s l a g e r ,   s t o p !" and whisked Boyton's learned pages right into his face, taking care at the same moment to administer a vigorous push to the long arm of the lever conveniently made by his basket.

This forced him to revolve suddenly on his own axis—beefsteak and all; and, as he spun round, I accelerated his motion with a pat or two from the '**c o m p e n d i u m**'. It was all the work of an instant, and executed just in time. The grammatical caress foiled his aim completely, and he flung his missile blindly in the wrong direction.

As I slipped unostentatiously into the crowd out of the immediate neighbourhood of the discomfited marksman, I had the satisfaction of seeing the dear old lady recover colour and smile. The babies crowed with delight, and clapped their hands. They thought it was a game got up for their special benefit!

THE OUTCOME OF A REVOLUTION.

I raised my hat and retired, a warm glow of self-approval in my breast, and on my lips an involuntary quotation from Boyton: "De spraakkunst is voor iedereen onmisbaar."

Meantime the brickbat fell harmlessly on the back of a policeman who, with hands tightly clasped behind him, was studying a bed of scarlet geraniums.

He never even turned, but only said "Ja, ja," over his shoulder!

Two days after this adventure my eye caught the following paragraph among the advertisements in the Nieuwe Courant:

"Stop, Slager, stop!"

The Baroness X. and her three grandchildren herewith beg heartily to thank the young Englishman for his gallant conduct in the Wood, on the 31st Ultimo.

CHAPTER VII.

A GOSSIPY LETTER.

"Don't talk any more about that grammar-book," I interposed. "It's all very well in its way, but it doesn't account for half Jack's adventures. Now I can let you into a secret. Please don't look so apprehensive, O'Neill! As it happens, I had a descriptive letter from Enderby just about the time that Jack was making the most brilliant progress with his Dutch vocabulary. It gave me a vivid picture of what was going on in the Hague when this linguist of ours got really started to work.

O'NEILL AS A GUIDE.

Here are two of these long epistles. In the first he tells me all about the MacNamaras—Jack's cousins, you know—who came across from Kilkenny, for a trip to Holland. They were at the Oude Doelen when he wrote, and our friend Jack was posing as a great Dutch scholar and showing them the sights.

(From Enderby to Cuey-na-Gael)
Doelen Hotel,
The Hague.

My dear Cuey-na-Gael,

You would be amazed to see the confidence with which O'Neill acts as guide to the MacNamaras.

MacNamara p è r e is mostly buried in museums, or is on the hunt for archaeological papers, so Kathleen and Terence are left on Jack's hands.

He has been everywhere with them, and has evidently impressed them with his astounding Dutch. To them it seems both correct and fluent. They have only had three days of it as yet, and haven't had time to find him out. Kathleen is as haughty as ever; and I can see she chafes at being obliged to submit to the direction of a mere boy, as she regards Jack.

She was furious the day before yesterday, when in passing through one of the back streets he asked her if she had ever noticed what the Dutch Government printed in front of the surgeries.

MEN MANGLED HERE.

She glanced up and, to her horror, read: "Hier mangelt men." It was only a momentary shock; she guessed soon enough what it meant; but it gave her a turn all the same. Perhaps it wasn't a very finished kind of joke, but she needn't have been quite so fierce about it.

"You're cruel," she said, "cruel and heartless! Why even your dogmatic and intolerable chum, Mr. van Leeuwen wouldn't have been so harsh as that."

Now it was that little speech of hers that suggested something to me. Was there ever anything between her and van Leeuwen? They were at the University about the same time, and it seems van Leeuwen was a great friend of the father, who had him down to his place in the country and showed him his manuscripts. But I believe Kathleen couldn't stand him. They used always to be arguing about the Suffragettes, and passed for official enemies, in a way,—at least as uncompromising leaders on opposite sides. She was fond of saying that van Leeuwen was a standing proof that mere learning couldn't enlarge the mind. Once in a private debate she referred to him as a "learned barbarian and a retrograde mediævalist."

NOUN HUNGER.

She was called to order for it, of course; but her apology didn't amount to much. She said she wouldn't mind dropping the adjectives, but she would stick to the nouns.

I believe van Leeuwen was quite content, however, and congratulated his witty antagonist on the fact that she would mellow with time.

We always thought in those days they were sworn foes, and always would be. But I have a dim idea there is now more friendly interest on both sides. And, by the way, van Leeuwen has been carrying on brisk correspondence with O'Neill, especially since he heard the MacNamaras were expected. He has offered his services, and those of his motor, to all and sundry, especially if they hail from Dublin: so I don't think he can be keeping up very much of a grudge.

But I was going to tell you about Jack.

Lately I had noticed that his Dutch vocabulary was growing very rich. He seemed to have quite a hunger for nouns, and he used to ask the names of everything. But I have no idea of what he was up to. To day I'll find out and write you.

Much haste. Yours as ever.
Enderby.

KINDSCH GEWORDEN.

(From Enderby to Cuey-na-Gael)

Dear Cuey,

I've just been at the Doelen Hotel—and the Macs are gone! Very sudden I must say. I suppose Kathleen has got tired of Holland; or is she trying to avoid van Leeuwen?

You see MacNamara m è r e had written me a friendly little note from Kilkenny, telling me that the Doctor—as she always calls her husband—had got a trifle absent-minded since his deafness became troublesome, and would I look him up occasionally during his stay in the Hague, and give him some advice about the Rhine.

Well, when I reached Vieux Doelen, the birds were flown. Gone at six o'clock, I was told—the three of them—to Cologne! Quick work, I thought; so I made a bee-line for O'Neill's. He surely would know about this sudden departure.

And in any case I wanted to get a glimpse of his new mysterious studies.

Just fancy! The landlady met me at the door with tears in her eyes.

A ROMMEL.

"O Mijnheer, Mijnheer!" she exclaimed half-sobbing. "Ik vrees voor mijnheer O'Neill. Hij studeert te veel, of ik weet het niet—maar het is niet goed met hem. Ik geloof", and here her voice sank to a horrified whisper, "dat hij een beetje kindsch geworden is; want hij heeft speelgoed gekocht, en hij maak overal zoo een rommel."

"Ja, juffrouw," I strove to explain, "Mijnheer studeert natuurlijk."

But she persisted, "Oh mijnheer! studeeren is het niet. Hij ziet het scherm voor een kachel aan, en verknoeit alles. Ik ben zoo bang, zoo benauwd! Ik durf het huis niet uit, van Maandag af al!"

Rather flustered by all this, I promised to call the doctor if it were necessary; then climbed up the stairs to O'Neill's door.

All was still. I knocked and entered. What a sight met my eyes! Indeed it was enough to astonish more experienced people than the landlady.

HOME-MADE BERLITZ.

Neatly fastened on one side of the table was a model train, engine and all. Beside it was a toy house, with yard, garden, and stiff wooden trees. Then there was a bit of a doll's room with a kitchen stove. And verily to every one of these articles there was a label affixed.

There sat the student, pen in hand, with a dictionary and a gum-bottle at his elbow. Snippets of paper littered his writing-desk and the floor around. His unfinished lunch (labelled too) looked down reproachfully from a pile of books built on the table.

Over the gorgeous screen that hid the hearth a conspicuous card was hung, bearing the mystic inscription, "What ought to be here—Kachel."

No wonder the careful hospita was upset. It would have been hard to say whether the apartment was more like a museum or an auction room.

He glanced up with a sort of blush when I came near; but raised his hand to enjoin silence, as he found the word he was in search of, and wrote it down.

Half expecting to see prices marked, I examined some of the labels.

Nearly every thing had its Dutch name gummed on to it, such as 'spiegel lijst,' 'behangsel,' 'schotel of bakje,' and even on his sleeve 'mouw van mijn jas.'

"It's all right!" he burst forth enthusiastically. "Doing Berlitz Dutch, you see! Self-taught, too! Splendid plan. Three hundred words a day. I'll have two thousand new nouns at my fingers' ends before the Macs are back from the Drachenfels. Precious few things in the ordinary way of life, I won't know then! Eh, what?"

SPOORWEG BEPALINGEN.

Then it dawned upon me he was getting up vocabulary.

"Nouns, of course," he said. "All nouns. That's the secret. True basis of any language.

"It's a discovery of my own. If you know the names of two or three thousand material things, you can never be at a loss. But I stick in a proverb, too, here and there, wherever it comes handy. See?"

He held up the sleeve of his dressing-gown on which the candid announcement was made in bold round-hand: "Ik heb het achter de mouw", and pointed to his bread-knife, which was tastefully adorned with the words: "Het mes op de keel zetten."

Yes, I saw.

Well; then he explained, and argued, and tried to proselytize me. He was making hay while the sun shone—which meant that he was preparing, in the absence of Terence and Kathleen, for his famous cycling-tour; getting on his armour, in fact.

In such spirits I had never seen him.

And, I must say, he made out a good case for his method. It seems he had anticipated most of the queries he might be obliged to put during his travels. He had docketed every part of a railway carriage, and even mastered all sorts of regulations, from those of the Luxe-trein to Buurtverkeer, and from the yearly ticket to the humble perronkaartje. It looked very thorough, and I understood that he had treated his cycle the same way. But I have grave doubts! I am the more confirmed in my scepticism from what the landlady told me at the door. After reassuring her on the score of O'Neill's health, I emphasised the fact that he was going on a trip, and must practise Dutch by way of preparation.

THE GROOTE WATER-BAAS.

That was worse than all, she thought; as Mijnheer O'Neill would certainly come to harm. "Hij is zoo veranderd! Hè! Het is zoo eng."

Yesterday he had asked her about the print of a sea-fight that her little boy had put up in the hall. She said it was de Ruyter; and began to expatiate on that hero's achievements.

But he cut her short with: "Een beroemde man was hij zeker; misschien de grootste *water-baas* van zijn tijd."

I explained that he probably meant *zee-held;* but not remembering the right term in time, had taken one like it.

But the landlady could not be pacified.

"Het doet mij huiveren te denken dat hij op reis gaat!" she said.

TWO THOUSAND NEW WORDS.

I was not without my apprehensions either. For he means to start out next week with two thousand new words.

He'll probably find that such hastily acquired information is not without its drawbacks.

But more again.
Vale, vale.
As ever yours,
Phil Enderby.

P. S. The Macs are gone to Bonn, where your uncle expects to find wonderful manuscripts. Not much fun for Kathleen though! And Terence will be bored to death. Why doesn't O'Neill bring him back to Holland and show him Amsterdam and other towns?

CHAPTER VIII.

THE SURPRISES OF THE MAAS.

"Well, well!" ejaculated O'Neill irritably. "What an inveterate old gossip Enderby is, to be sure!

"Of course I got Terence back quite soon from Bonn, where he had nothing to do; and I gave him a splendid time sight-seeing in Haarlem and Amsterdam. I'll tell you about that, another time.

But first about my run to Rotterdam, where I went one day for a little change I needed.

The landlady was a bit peevish and hysterical, and, of course, very bothersome. She never quite took to the Berlitz method, as I had improved it; and she became grandmotherly to me from the moment I made that slip about the *zee-held*.

The whole thing was getting on her nerves, so I gave her a rest. Took a day off, in fact; and went for a tour round the Rotterdam havens.

FAIRYLAND.

I had some idea of recapitulating the old ground—the first thousand words, you know—whilst I should be steaming around the harbour. But as soon as we pushed off from the wharf and went skimming over the sun-lit Maas, the brilliant and animated scene wiped the new vocabulary clean out of my mind for the time-being; and I didn't feel at all inclined to dig it out of my notes.

The marvellous colouring of everything held me spell-bound. It was like fairyland. Our boat was crowded, and a man on board pointed out the sights. That was the only Dutch study I got that day; for some one began to speak to me in English—an Amsterdammer, as it appeared, who told me that the grachten in Amsterdam surpassed every other spectacle the world had to show; and made me promise to go and see them as soon as I could.

I asked him what he thought of the harbour we were in; but he wasn't so enthusiastic.

Meantime it had grown darker, and a steady, cold, sea-fog drifted round us. It got dismally wet, as well as gloomy; and the deck dripped with clammy moisture. We were hardly moving, presently; and our captain kept the steam whistle hard at work. The sight-seers were grievously disappointed;

and one fellow-victim informed me it would be a good thing if we got near land anywhere, in time to catch the last train.

IK KRIJSCH, IK FLUIT EN IK GIL.

Horns kept booming around us, every few seconds; perky little tugs and immense black hulls swept by us at arm's length, piping or bellowing, according to their temperament and ability.

The Amsterdammer and I had gone to the prow, to try and peer a little further into the dense curling vapour, when a siren—I think that's what you call the thing—gave such a sudden blood-curdling yell at our very elbow, it seemed as if we had trodden on the tail of the true and original Sea-serpent, and that the reptile was shrieking in agony.

From that time on, we had sea-serpents every other minute—whole swarms of them—infuriated, inquisitive or resigned—soprano, alto, tenor;—all whining, hooting and snorting; every one trying to howl all the others down.

Excuse my referring to it, but it was the best illustration I had yet got of Boyton's verbs.

"Ik graauw, ik kef en ik kweel!" said one set of voices. "Ik krijsch, ik fluit en ik gil!" answered their rivals.

POLYPHEMUS AND THE SEA-SERPENT.

But the deep boom of new-comers swept the earlier songsters out of the field: "Ik rammel, ik ratel en ik scheur". It was a regular chorus.

"Ik gier en ik piep", squeaked the little tugs, "ik fop en ik jok".

But the first musicians—the sentimental ones—wouldn't be outdone. They were evidently turning over their grammars very rapidly, to get a really melancholy selection, for in another moment their lugubrious snuffle pierced the fog like a knife: "Ik wee-ee-een; ik krijt; en ik hui-ui-ui-l-l!"

There was one long-drawn-out sob, that rose and fell and rose again with such appalling and expressive anguish that I could have imagined half the Netherlands had turned into a gigantic sea-serpent, and had bitten off its own tongue. So human, too, was its tortured wail, that I instinctively thought of Polyphemus having his eye gouged out by Ulysses. The hero, you remember, did it with a burning pine. One has a horrible sympathy for Polyphemus, even though he is a monster and mythical.

Happily our Polyphemus only gave two or three of his prize yells. Then he seemed to settle into sleep, away down the river somewhere.

CLOTHO.

The Amsterdam-man explained to me that in his city the fog-horns were much more musical.

This thesis was warmly contested by a Rotterdammer who had overheard it, and who spoke of the Capital with a distinct want of reverence.

The argument soon deviated into Dutch, and I lost hold of it; but through a cloud of statistics and history I observed that local patriotism on both sides stood at fever heat.

By and by, the fog thinned a little; and we crept along to a landing-stage, where the Amsterdammer and I climbed on shore with alacrity. We lost our way at first, and wandered about within earshot of the siren-brood, whooping and calling and taunting one another on the river; but my new-made friend stumbled at last on some spot he was acquainted with; and hastily giving me some directions, went off to his train.

After the long Polyphemus-concert on the murky river I wasn't in much humour for Dutch, but I had to speak it at every corner to ask my way.

In an open thoroughfare—there were some people about, but not many—near an archway, I came upon Clotho.

GLOOM AND MYSTERY.

Perhaps the Greek Mythology was running in my head: but there she sat. Old beyond words, but hale; wrapped up marvellously with head and jaws swathed in dim flannel, she gazed, without moving, on a table in front of her, spread with dried eels and other occult delicacies. As I approached, to enquire for the 'kortste weg naar de electrische tram', she didn't move a muscle. Something about her made me pause upon my step, and refrain from speech.

No movement.

But wait! One thickly muffled hand went out to some obscure eatable, slowly grasped it, dipped it in a sort of cup, then, still more slowly, brought it to her lips.

Yes. She was alive; for she munched, calmly and dispassionately.

The sight impressed me. It was like Fate; or an ancient priestess performing mysterious rites. Clotho would look like this, if Clotho would munch instead of spin.

Meantime the inevitable butcher's boy had joined me. Two of them, indeed, stood at my side, curious to know what interested the vreemdeling.

The old lady never winced under the scrutiny, but put forth her hand again for another shell.

WHAT IS TREK?

There was a book-stall near, but nobody at it, as far as I could see. The whole street sounded hollow; and everything dripped. It made me shiver to look at the stone-pillars, oozy and moist, with condensed sea-fog trickling down. The glaring street-lamps hardly lit up the scene; but they showed the damp. Polyphemus gave a distant whoop, as if it were his last: and the Spectre munched. She hadn't once looked up.

It all felt like a dream—except for the butchers' boys.

"Wat doet ze—die oude mejuffrouw?" I enquired.

"Ze zit te eten," was the prompt reply.

"Waarom zit ze te eten daar?" I asked.

"Om dat ze trek heeft!"

A snigger went round the company. Evidently that reply was of the nature of wit; and they expected something sparkling from me in return.

B u t I couldn't sparkle.

THE SOCRATIC DIALOGUE.

"T r e k " was unknown to me. Strange, how you can be bowled over by a simple word, if you've never heard it. Trekken—trok—getrokken, was familiar. That meant 'to pull,' 'draw,' or 'wander'. "Trekschuit"—"trekpot"—"trekvogel"; I had them all labelled on my desk in the Hague. But "trek" itself, what was that exactly? Provided of course, the youth were grammatical,—which I very much doubted.

"Zij heeft getrokken," however, when I tried it, only raised new difficulties. **W h a t** then did she pull, and **w h y** ?

'Trekvogel' was an alluring idea to follow up, in a town where Jan Olieslagers' fame was universal: but common sense forbade my pursuing that line far.

The defects of my home-made Berlitz became painfully evident. It's humiliating, when you have your 2000 new nouns at your fingers' ends, and hundreds of old ones; and yet can't understand the first thing a k n e c h t says.

But the bystanders were growing impatient; so—to withdraw gracefully—I enquired, "wat is *trek?*"

It was probably the best retort I could have made. "Ja, wat is het?" he soliloquised, evidently puzzled, "Ik weet het niet. Maar ik heb altijd trek."

"Ik ook", said a smaller boy; "in een boterham."

Tongues were loosened on all sides. "Nee; in een lekker stuk worst," I heard one say.

"Nee; niet waar"; interrupted a brawny fellow with a brick-red face; "Zuurkool en spek."

A COSY TALK.

I nipped the unprofitable discussion in the bud by demanding, as I moved away: "Maar wat *is* trek?"

"Dat weet je wel," said the first fellow, the wit. "Als je te veel eet."

"Nee, heelemaal niet," jeered a late-comer. "Kan je begrijpen! Maar als je **n i e t s** eet, **d a n** heb je trek!"

The crowd cheered at this. He had evidently the majority with him. High words followed; and the controversy became general, as the protagonists in this psychological debate found backers, and swarmed away towards the centre of town.

I was left alone, and Clotho looked up.

She dipped a periwinkle in one of the weird cups, and held it towards me.

"Heeft Mijnheer trek?" Would I join in the repast!

"Ik? Duizendmaal verschooning!" I said, as I quickened my pace in rapid retreat.

My confusion increased as I reflected that I had probably been urging my late interlocutors to "define appetite"—a thing even Aristotle could hardly do. Naturally the populace broke into parties—Aristotelians and Platonists (let us say), or into Hoekschen en Kabeljauwschen.

THE CHAT.

In any case my confidence was shaken in my improved, home-made Berlitz. It might be splendid for travelling; but in ordinary life it didn't seem to cover the ground.

On arriving at my lodgings I was met at the door by the landlady's son. He was beaming. Lately he had been working up his English, and truly had made giant strides.

"Koot eeffening, Sir," he said; "Koot eeffening! Ai hef an little chat." "**I w i s h   t o   h a v e   a   c h a t**", he *seemed* to mean.

It was an odd request for a trifling practice in English; but I like to encourage merit, so I assured him of my willingness to have a friendly talk.

"Oh, yes. All right," I said. "But won't you come up stairs? We have a few minutes before supper."

"But—Ai hef **h e r e** an naiz little chat!"

"Ah, just so. Did you perhaps have a talk with some one in English when I was away?"

"No, sir; but ai *hef* een chat."

This was bewildering; and as he seemed puzzled, too, and always stuck to the same noun I investigated more fully.

"You talk of a *chat!*—dat is een praatje, weet je wel?"

EVIDENCES OF HUNGER.

"Nee, mijnheer, heus: het is waar. Geen praatje."

We were half-way up the stairs now. "Come on", I said.

"Vayt", he replied, diving into some recess. "Ai vil let see you."

In an instant he was back with something under his coat. This he produced with the delighted exclamation: "ze little chat!"

It was a bedraggled kitten that he had discovered wandering about in the fog and mewing piteously. "Vil you hef him? Anders, zegt moe, hij kan niet blijven."

"I'll talk to your mother about the kitten," I answered. "Kitten,—that's what we call it—not chat. Maar hoor eens, jongen, heeft het poesje trek?"

"O mijnheer, verbazend!" was the ecstatic reply; and in another three minutes he had a saucer of milk under the foundling's nose, and was watching kitty's lapping operations with a joy as keen as that of kitty herself.

I had got what I wanted without any philosophic argument. There was the proof.

Trek is *appetite*.

CHAPTER IX.

THE THUNDERSTORM.

I must tell you about that great walk we took from Leyden to Haarlem. That was just after Terence came back from Germany, wearied with waiting till his learned Dad would cease pottering about the museums in Bonn.

He wrote to van Leeuwen in Arnhem; and urged that youth use his influence with the University Librarian to let Dr. MacNamara see the Irish manuscripts he was so keen upon. Then, if you please, my brave Terence thought his duties were over, as far as helping his father was concerned. Taking the next train for the Hague he turned up unexpectedly at my lodgings.

That was at six in the morning, and he banged at my bedroom door till I was awake.

THE NORTH SEA COAST.

"I'm back," he said: "And I'm going to carry you off on that famous bicycle tour of yours. Hurry up with all those papers and preparations and things,—and I'll be round with my bike in no time!"

"Well!" I shouted through the closed door, "you may come as soon as ever you like; but there'll be no bicycle tour to-day. I'm not nearly ready yet. I've all the nouns from T to Z to learn yet; and it'll take me another week. Catch me leaving this neighbourhood without those nouns! No, my boy. But I'll take a tramp with you to the seaside, if you like."

He didn't wait for my explanations but pranced off grumbling, and I didn't see him till noon. He was then quite willing to fall in with my project of a long walk—first by the strand to Noordwijk, then inland through the dunes, and so on to Haarlem.

We only got as far as Noordwijk that evening. After a heavy miserable trudge by the shore, and mostly through loose sand, we were glad enough to put up at Huis-ter-Duin for the night. The sunset, magnificent though it was, could hardly banish the deep sleepiness that seized us. Terence, who was in better training than I, sat up smoking a while, but I heard him go off to his room before I fell over. All the music, laughter, and talk about the place, never in the slightest degree disturbed our slumber.

AN EXQUISITE DAWN.

I slept like a log, and awoke early, with the sound of the sea in my ears. It was a softly modulated, gentle murmur that seemed to call me; and when I looked out, the view was superb. Deep blue, almost indigo in hue, and calm as oil, the waves stood high on the sands. Every now and then a long, knife-like billow would slowly rise up for half-a-mile or so, poise itself for an instant, and then fall with a mighty flap, like a wall of slate. Away out towards the horizon the ocean gleamed a fairy-like blue and opal; but close at hand it had a deep, menacing tint that took your breath away. And all the time those slatey ledges of water kept languidly lifting themselves and suddenly dropping, as if they were alive.

When I opened the window, a cool wind softly stole in—like some subtle elixir. I looked at my watch. It was half past four. Fired with the idea of having a tramp by that mysterious light, I went off and roused Terence—happily without terrifying the other inmates of the hotel. He was willing to make an early start if I could secure him enough breakfast.

A MORNING WALK.

This required some diplomacy. Suddenly encountering a *knecht* prowling about and collecting boots, I tried to communicate our plans to him, and gain his sympathy. No idiom, however, that I was acquainted with was equal to this strain: so I had recourse to the language of gesture and the display of coin. This at last induced him to bring us part of his own modest breakfast—a chunk of black bread and a hard-boiled egg—and to let us out by the front door.

He kept our bags, however, and a bankbiljet, to settle the rekening provisionally, and as an evidence of good faith. It was a fussy business getting him to agree even to this, and in consequence I quite forgot about my dictionary and "walking-tour notes"—which were strapped up in the bag.

Indeed, I didn't notice the neglect till we were far away from the hotel. But there was no Dutch needed for a long time.

It was an exhilarating experience to go careering along by that weird, threatening sea in the fresh morning air. The scent of herbs and wild-flowers on the dunes greeted us when we took a turn inland: and the colours of everything around us kept changing with incredible swiftness.

BY THE SUMMER SEA.

At first we couldn't keep our eyes off the mirror-like expanse of water. Its slate became steel-blue—the steel-blue deepened into purple shading off into amethyst, while the sky and the air all about us grew rosy, then saffron, then silver.

Over and across the rolling hills we trudged, our spirits rising every instant. Why shouldn't we keep on till we got opposite Haarlem, then strike off east, do that city, and return by rail? Why not indeed? Huis-ter-Duin and its slippered knecht could settle the matter of the rekening and the change, by post; and we should make a day of it!

So we climbed up and down along the edge of the grassy slopes, till the tide retired from the sands a little. There we had a delightful hour, along the firm damp shore. It grew sultry after a while; yet it was only a quarter to eight. There would be more heat yet! Alternately we tried the dunes and the beach—the beach and the dunes—but there was no shelter from the sun; and the pleasant wind had died down. After an other couple of hours' toil through the hot, loose sand we decided we had enough of the coast for the day, and followed a kind of winding path inland. This was a regular cart-track at first, and promised to lead us to some thriving village where we could have a rest. But it didn't. It twined round a score of scattered potatoe plots, and then came to an abrupt and ignominious end against a wire fence, on the top of a hill. No doubt we ought to have gone back and kept along the shore. But we were too hungry to think of returning to the desolation we had left. What we wanted was to see houses as soon as possible—houses containing eatables and cool rooms and chairs. Besides, we were as yet pretty confident of our geographical whereabouts; accordingly we pushed on for Haarlem—as we thought.

LOST IN THE DUNES.

Well, it was a great mistake! The map makes the dunes only a few miles broad at most, yet we climbed up and down for hours, and couldn't get clear of them.

Once we saw a fisherman at a distance and we yelled to him. He answered "terug" very faintly, and waved both arms. We hurried to meet him, but not a trace of him was to be found. Though the heat was intense, after a while shimmery haze began to spread over the sky, and there came a sudden change. It got dark and cold; and the storm that had been threatening all day burst on us with fury. In two or three minutes we were drenched. There was a marvellous display of sheet lightning so curious and varied that for a while it diverted our attention from our miserable plight, as we stumbled on over soaked hillocks and sand. We had a good hour of this.

NO FOOD FOR SALE.

In a dismal grove of non-descript-shrubs, we at last stumbled upon a trifling shelter, just as the rain was ceasing; and there we shivered like aspens, till the truth dawned upon us that there was a faint sound of human voices over the slope. "Hurrah!" we shouted. "Relief at last—and a chance of something to eat!"

Stiff and dripping though we were, we positively bounded over the sand hill.

Two or three small one-storied cottages came soon into view. Rushing into the first—it looked like a shop, and had the words *garen en band* over the window—we demanded pointedly if we could get food. The youngish woman who ambled slowly to and fro behind the counter, said she had no coffee or bread for us, but we could get these things in Haarlem. There was a good restaurant there.

"Geen ei?" I asked.

No; not even an egg for sale.

AN ORDINARY BAKER.

Very disappointed we retired, still dripping, and gloomier than ever; but as we left the winkel I espied a group of schoolchildren, with capes round their heads, dancing along merrily hand in hand. They were evidently coming from school. Such bright blue eyes, such plump and rosy cheeks suggested that food was plentiful wherever they lived. There must be a butcher and a baker near, I concluded; and by a happy inspiration I turned back to the depressing *garen en band* shop, and enquired where the local baker was to be found.

"Is er een baker hier?" I enquired politely of the lethargic juffrouw.

She woke up immediately. "Ja, zeker!" was the prompt reply. "Net gisteren thuis gekomen!"

This was all right, of course. Why does he come home and go away, I wondered. But, after all, that was a small matter. He was at home now. A peripatetic baker, perhaps, might be some very special and clever artist in pies and tarts and rich cake—and it was the humble, ordinary baker that we were in search of. I stated this. "Geen banket baker is noodig, juffrouw!" I explained. "Een gewonen baker bedoel ik—een gewonen alledaagschen baker. Bestaat er een hier?"

THE BROKEN SIESTA.

She had meantime summoned two young men from a sort of den behind the shop, and now communicated my wishes to them with an interest and an animation that I hadn't expected. They led us rapidly half a mile across fields, and then up a little lane. The last few yards were done in good record time, I should say.

This sympathetic promptitude we highly appreciated, as we felt now more and more famished, the nearer we approached provisions. We reached the baker's house breathless, and were ushered panting into a kind of waiting room. At least you couldn't call it a shop exactly.

When the baker came into this apartment (by the way it was a woman, that turned up—a portly and middle-aged woman) we noticed that she was rather dishevelled, as if just awakened from a much needed siesta. I was sorry, but not surprised. Bakers are often that way, you know. They bake during the night, and sleep during the day. Thus they are rather drowsy and cross, if you wake them up. She looked both. There was a portentous frown upon her brow; and really, she seemed somewhat of the virago type. That made me doubly polite.

"Duizendmaal vergiffenis, banketbaker!" I apologised with my best bow. "Het spijt mij geweldig.—Maar zult gij zoo goed willen zijn—?"

WOU JE ETEN?

"Ja ja!" she interrupted impatiently; "Waar? Heb je een rijtuig?"

"Een rijtuig?" I exclaimed in bewilderment. "Nee. Ik heb geen rijtuig. Maar mag ik u beleefd verzoeken of U zoo goed—."

"Ja, ja! Is er haast bij?" She broke in again.

"Wel zeker!" I replied courteously, "Veel haast. Wij zijn verbazend hongerig."

But she was gone, and hadn't heard the last remark. In a moment or two she reappeared, fully dressed, tying the strings of her bonnet.

As I waited a second before repeating my request, she grew most unreasonably irritable, and actually stamped her foot, exclaiming disrespectfully: "Gaauw nouw! gaauw een beetje."

"Ja baker!" I answered. "Wilt gij zoo goed zijn, twee boterhammetjes en twee glaasjes melk te brengen?"

She stopped titivating herself at the mirror, and turning round groaned in a voice of horror: "Wou je eten?"

"Ja," I contrived to put in, as politely as I could; "als U zoo goed wilt zijn."

BETAALD ZETTEN.

"Maar schaam jullie niet? bent jullie kinderen dat je nouw om een boterham moet vragen?"

It was plain she was a good deal ruffled. Accordingly to appease and conciliate her I smiled again, and said deferentially: "Het heeft niets te beduiden. Wij moeten een heel klein boterhammetje gebruiken. Een sneedje brood zonder iets—dat is ook goed."

She seemed stunned by this harmless announcement; and I deemed it prudent to offer her a bribe of some kind. The simplest plan was to promise to pay her well for any trifle we took.

"Het is een kleinigheid," I told her—"niets dan een kleinigheid. Maar ik zal het je betaald zetten."

That loosened her tongue. Her natural fluency asserted itself and appeared to fine advantage. But she was so needlessly excited that I knew there must be a misunderstanding somewhere. Accordingly to remove all haziness I just indicated that she had failed to grasp my meaning. The idiom for this I fortunately recollected. *You don't quite follow* was one of those choice specimens of local colour that, by frequent repetition, I had thoroughly imprinted on my memory.

YOU DON'T QUITE FOLLOW.

"Duizendmaal verschooning," I said heartily, "bent U soms niet goed snik?"

The effect of this well meant apology was electrical. The woman really became very rude. She got pale and grabbed at a chair. As we withdrew unostentatiously, we noticed her springing in our direction and talking. It was the most fluent talk I had yet heard in Dutch. She did not hesitate one instant for gender, number, or case. It rained, hailed and stormed terrible words—werkwoorden, voorzetsels, and especially tusschenwerpsels.

Terence and I ran.

On reaching safety outside Terence asked me: "What was she angry about?"

"Oh," I answered, "as likely as not it's something out of the grammar. I believe I didn't use the right idiom. You have to be very particular about these things, you see.

I said vragen *voor* een boterham, I think; and it should be vragen *om*. Still she made far too big a fuss over it: and I'd tell her so, if I could."

When we got outside of her garden plot and had latched the gate behind us, I turned to wave our grammarian a graceful adieu.

REPARTEE UNDER DIFFICULTIES.

"Baker!" I said. "Banket baker! Wees niet zoo kleinzeerig. Niet zoo kwaalijknemend hoor! Wij zijn niet tegen je opgewassen. Maar",—and here

I sank my voice to a confidential whisper, to make the irrelevancy sound as like wit as possible,—"maar, U weet nooit hoe een koe een haas vangt!"

I still flatter myself that the exit was worthy of the occasion.

CHAPTER X.

THE DEVOTED NURSE.

"Wel," continued Jack; "it was these experiences that made me begin to doubt the value of my Berlitz soliloquy-method. But Terence helped me to give the system a really good trial; and he worked as hard as I did.

It was quite different with Kathleen. When she came back from Germany, she was keen on art, but apparently had been moping about something. And she refused to study any more Dutch.

That was before the accident, you see. After that, she was quite angelic and nursed her father assiduously, and the landlady's little son, too.

AN ACCIDENT.

You know, of course, that uncle got a severe shock from a motor-bike along the canal. Jan who had been prowling around, to give his "chat" an airing, ran across just in time to push the absent-minded old gentleman out of the way. But the lad was thrown on the ground and badly hurt. Uncle pulled round soon enough—his indignation at the motor cyclist helped him, as he had some vague idea, if he were up and about, he could get the culprit arrested. But Jan grew steadily worse for the first week. The violent fall and the bruise were both very bad for the plucky youngster.

Kathleen kept going back and forward, looking after the sufferers. She said she never could repay Jan enough for saving her father's life. It appears to have been a 'close shave', at the edge of that deep canal; and Uncle nearly had them all in.

THE SUITOR'S MISTAKE.

As a matter of fact, he had spent the morning with me, telling me about his grand 'find' of original Celtic manuscripts in Germany, and about van Leeuwen's kindness. I never saw him so taken with anybody! In Bonn he had got wind of these precious Celtic relics; and, as everything was closed at the University at that time of the year, he worried and fumed, till he met some of the authorities that knew van Leeuwen. Immediately he had banged off a telegram to Arnhem, requesting van Leeuwen's private influence; and, to his delight, that young man came joyfully in person. Of course he would! It was too good a chance to be missed. Indeed it was just the opportunity he wanted. And yet he and Kathleen quarrelled fiercely over trifles all the time.

But I was telling you about my uncle's escape. It seems he was ambling along in his usual oblivious style, on the sunny side of the street, when he stopped (no doubt painfully near the edge of the canal) to note down something that occurred to him for his book. Just then a motor-cycle turned the corner at a fiendish speed, and was nearly over him. Uncle is the most helpless of mortals at such times—and he was stepping hurriedly into the canal, when Jan bounded across the road and pulled him right.

The bike-tourist must have been a heartless fellow; for he never swerved, but bore down at full tilt on both rescuer and rescued, while they were still on the edge of the water.

The youthful Jan, however, is both original and daring; for he turned the motor man aside as cleverly as if he had Boyton in his hand.

NO DUTCH NEEDED.

He either flung himself or his cap against the advancing horror. Terence says it was the kitten he threw. In any case the little fellow did, as a last resource, try to protect both his dear kitty and the Engelschen Mijnheer, at some risk to himself. The "chat" was unharmed, but fled up an adjacent elm, whence it had to be coaxed down at dusk with endless saucerfuls of milk.

This task Kathleen took on herself, after we discovered that Dr. MacNamara, though shaken, was not injured. Nothing would have pleased you better than to have seen her beaming face as she brought the trembling little kitty to Jan's bedside. She didn't know a word of Dutch; but managed to communicate quite easily, by signs, with Jan's mother, whom she promised to come often and see.

We all assumed, at first, that the little fellow had escaped scot-free; but, in a day or two, he was in high fever, and unconscious. He had got a contusion, the doctor said, and would be confined to his cot for weeks.

It was marvellous to see how Kathleen comforted the poor mother, without either grammar, Polite Dialogue, or the use of Het.

JAN'S INCOHERENCES.

I grew quite jealous and envious. Here was I who had been slaving at syntax and accidence for weeks, and I couldn't carry on an intelligent conversation for two minutes without deviating into metaphysics, or getting into a quarrel; while my cousin (who said she hated Dutch) could get through the niceties of sick-room nursing, and the subtleties of heartening up the poor hysterical mother, with the utmost ease and success.

And I knew for certain that she couldn't go through the Present Optative of 'ik graauw, ik kef en ik kweel', or give one of the rules for gij (lieden)— no, not to save her life. But she was never at a loss, for all that. A more devoted nurse, indeed, I cannot imagine.

At the crisis, when the little sufferer was really in danger, she used to watch by him hours at a stretch, to relieve the helpless mother.

The serious turn came all at once; and no aid was at hand. Jan was in pain, and wandered in his talk, crying out that the motor-fiets was hunting him into the canal, for having rescued a v r e e m d e l i n g ; and pouring forth such a torrent of elementary English and Boyton-Dutch as surprised us all.

I fancy it was, in part, my early translations he had treasured up; for some of my mistakes about handcuffs and dogcollars figured amid the incoherences; and it was pitiable to hear him plead for a z i e b e n e d e n to wrap round his injured arm—already bandaged as tightly as he could bear it.

EEN STUK OF EEN.

Then he kept ringing the changes on an expression I must have used in argument with his mother the day I persuaded her to keep his bedraggled foundling.

"Het is geen menigte poesjes, zegt Mijnheer; het is maar een stuk of een. Heus, moe, laat hem blijven. Niet bang, hoor, schattie, je bent maar een stuk of een! Pas op, Mijnheer, daar komt de fiets!" And so on d a c a p o .

So wild and restless was he, the second evening of the fever, that we had to summon the doctor unexpectedly, quite late.

Yes; his condition was disquieting, and we must get him to sleep. It was largely a matter of nursing, at the moment; new medicine was sent for; his head was to be kept cool; and only one watcher was to remain in the room. Above all, no noise. If the English juffrouw, who seemed to understand the lad's state, would consent to sit up to two or three o'clock, so much the better. The excited mother could have a rest meantime. Otherwise she would be fit for nothing next day.

KITTY GIVES KOPJES.

But no sooner had the good doctor softly closed the front door, than my landlady declared it was her intention to watch all night.

Kathleen was at her wits' end. In vain did she make signs and talk emphatic English in her high voice, or try coaxing with a bit of the brogue. All her feminine free-masonry failed to communicate the faintest idea to the mother.

Uncle MacNamara, who had been waiting to take his daughter back to the Doelen, tried moral suasion in his own particular brand of German, and even in other tongues.—Terence says his father recited a well-known passage from the Iliad in his eagerness to be persuasive!—But all without avail. She wouldn't heed anybody; and she wouldn't go; she sat close to the cot, rocking violently to and fro, and moaning "Mijn eigen kind! mijn eigen kind!"

The little fevered face was puckered with a new perplexity at the sound of all this grief and the familiar voice.

"Moeder," he cried, "moederr! Daar komt ie weer! Hij wou me in 't water gooien. Moeder, vasthoue, hoor!"

It was most painful; for my landlady's impending hysterics were making the lad worse every moment.

A QUIET SLEEP.

"Is poesje ook weggeloopen?" he said presently. A happy thought struck Kathleen. She stole downstairs, and presently returned with the 'chat', which was purring vigorously and giving 'kopjes'.

As she placed the soft furry creature in Jan's hands, he stopped moaning and stroked it joyfully. "Dag, Kitty!" he said with delight. "Ben je terug?"

Apparently he thought it was I who had restored the wanderer, for he explained: "Geen praatje, mijnheer: Zat is mine naiz litle chat."

Then, exhausted and satisfied, he dropped into a sound sleep.

CHAPTER XI.

GOSSIP AND DIPLOMACY.

The strain was over; and the little lad slumbered peacefully,—until dawn, as it proved. We got the mother gradually quieted, and at last induced to go off to bed, leaving Kathleen in charge for the night. About half-past-one, Terence and I, growing hungry, extemporised a sort of pic-nic in the kitchen; but Kathleen wouldn't touch anything we brought her.

It was then I began to notice how grave she was, and silent.

But I must say, nobody could be more devoted than she was to the youthful invalid.

He awoke rather early after his timely sleep, but much calmer. And—a good sign—he had a healthy 'trek', which we were gratified to see in operation upon 'beschuit' and 'melk', before his mother arrived to resume the reins of authority.

THE DISCOURAGED SUITOR.

As we escorted Kathleen to her hotel in the cool of the morning, we found her singularly irresponsive, not to say depressed; and I somehow got wind of the fact that van Leeuwen, who had motored up to the Hague, on hearing of her father's accident, had been prowling about the Vieux Doelen ever since. He had visited Dr. MacNamara almost every day; but Kathleen had kept studiously aloof.

"I know he likes father," she said, "and I'm glad he came so often to see him. Not very interesting, otherwise! In any case he has suddenly vanished into space!"

The evening before, when she was on her way to my landlady's to watch by the sick boy, van Leeuwen had met her right in front of the Mauritshuis. But she had treated him with such stately indifference, and greeted his remarks with such frigid courtesy, that the good-natured fellow was really hurt. He had in fact returned the same evening to Arnhem.

Kathleen said she was very glad, except for her father's sake. But she didn't give one the impression of being enthusiastic about it, and I drew my own conclusions.

WILL KATHLEEN STUDY DUTCH?

On reaching the Doelen, we found a hasty scrawl from the very man we had been talking of—van Leeuwen—inviting Terence and myself to a cycling tour in his neighbourhood.

"Well, then, I'll go next Friday," Terence broke out; "at least, if you're ready then, Jack. We'll have a grand time. Dad is all right now; and that funny little kid is on the mend. So we can go with a clear conscience. Say, yes."

"Ah, that's like you boys", said Kathleen banteringly, but without the ghost of a smile, "to go cycling about, enjoying yourselves, no matter what happens to others! I'm still anxious about that child. And I do wish I understood him better when he talks."

"As for that", I interrupted, "I'll give you the key to it, in an instant. Jan's reminiscences are all about my Dutch. Well, I'll lend you my diary, and the most entertaining Grammar in Holland. Besides, I've written a monograph on obvious blunders, English into Dutch. Read these, now, when you're tending this convalescent boy-hero of yours. He'll understand them, I'll be bound; and it'll shake him up, and do you a world of good yourself."

AN INTERESTING COACH.

"What a silly cousin, to be sure!" she replied. "You forget, sir, I need some one to explain all your double-Dutch. Get me a 'coach' now, a competent one, who knows everything, and I'll give your booklet a trial."

"Done!" I said, as we parted.

And I held her to it. My diary kept her amused for a couple of days, as she watched in the sick-room. It roused her out of her depression, and she got into the way of reading things to Jan as he recovered.

She couldn't remain quite smileless; but grew interested enough in Dutch to demand my monograph and—above all—the Grammar!

"You shall have them both," I assured her,—"the booklet on the spot; and the Grammar, when I get as far as Arnhem and don't need to use it for a while."

"Couldn't I have it sooner? I'm dying with curiosity to see that awful book. Or, when you are there, and any of your friends are coming to the Hague, just send it with them."

"Yes. There's a 'coach' coming up in a day or two. I'll send it along."

THE DIPLOMATIC EPISTLE.

I fancied her eyes gave a bit of a flicker. But she was meek and friendly: so I knew it was all right. She hadn't asked what kind of coach. But she's intelligent.

That very instant I went home and wrote van Leeuwen that we—Terence and I—were starting next day, by train, for Arnhem, whence we should have a run through Gelderland.

There was no note-paper in the house, but I couldn't wait. So I a penned what I had to say on a series of visiting cards,—numbering them: 1, 2, 3 up to 10, and enclosing them in a portly yellow envelope. It was the only thing I had. I was pleased to notice its impressive aspect, as that would prevent its getting lost readily.

For I attached much importance to that communication.

In it I prepared van Leeuwen's mind, indirectly and circuitously, for apprehending the idea that Miss MacNamara was now deeply interested in Dutch; and was studying it to help her in nursing that sick boy. Also that, as she had grown much too sombre of late with the responsibilities she had assumed, we were trying to brighten her up. When the lad was quite well, we should all do the Friesland meres, before we returned to Kilkenny. But not for a while yet.

THE BRINK OF A ROMANCE.

And so on. I hinted as distantly as I could, that he had motored back to Arnhem a trifle too soon. We were *all* sorry he had left so suddenly. Even yet, if he would leave his camera at home—the one with the loud click— and if he wouldn't be too exclusively immersed in Celtic manuscripts, and avoided arguing about the Suffragettes, when he did meet with the MacNamara family, there was no reason to suppose that his offences were beyond pardon. All this in shadowy outline—for fear he would motor up like a Fury, and either break his neck on the way, or spoil everything by premature action.

I made the haze quite thick, here and there, on the visiting cards—their form lent itself to obscurity—and I told him I should see him without fail within twenty-four hours.

"I might have to ask a favour at his hands about a grammar.

Terence was well: the Doctor was well, went to Leyden daily to the Library. We expected to reach Velperweg toward midday. Don't be out."

I posted the yellow missive with my own hands, and reckoned out by the 'bus-lichting' plate, that it would be collected that night.

WELL EARNED REPOSE.

"Tour or no tour, to-morrow," I said to myself, heaving a sigh of relief, after my race to the pillar-box; "We're on the brink of a romance, if the protagonists only knew it. A little bad Dutch now seems all that is required. And we can rely on Boyton."

Queer, when you think of it, that you sometimes hold people's destinies in the hollow of your hand!

However, I didn't philosophise much, but got to sleep as soon as ever I could,—content as from a good day's work.

CHAPTER XII.

A STUDY IN CHARACTER.

Next morning we were up at dawn to be in time for the first express. We cycled to the station; but a row of market-boats, that had reached the one and only canal-bridge on our route, kept us waiting till they filed past; and we missed our train.

"Choost kon!" exclaimed a porter cheerfully, as he took our cycles. "Day-train choost away—von—two—meenit—ako!"

"Never mind", I rejoined. "There are plenty of day-trains left. It's early yet."

As he looked doubtful, I added in the vernacular: "Wij zijn in goeje tijd voor den bommel; nie-waar? Zes vier en veertig."

"Net, mijnheer", he replied, grinning appreciation of my Dutch, as he led the way to the l o k e t .

AN UNWELCOME INTERRUPTION.

There were no difficulties there. You merely had to say. "Twee enkele reis, Arnhem. Tweede klasse. Gewone biljetten," and there you were. And these 'g e w o n e   b i l j e t t e n ' made the forwarding of the cycles simplicity itself.

Duly provided with the forthcoming f i e t s - p a p i e r t j e s   we ensconced ourselves in a non-smoker, and—to while away the time—rehearsed our Traveller's Dialogue. That is the system I had made out long since, but now partly forgotten. Terence had benefited by my tuition, and could now keep the ball rolling, with more or less relevant remarks, whilst I enumerated the parts of a train, and talked about tickets and towns.

So smoothly did our conversation run that we were tempted to repeat it with variations; and we were just in the middle of as fine an elocutionary practice as ever you heard, when there was a scramble on the platform; and in there bounded into our compartment—just as the train began to move off—three tourists, hot and breathless!

THE LINGUIST AND THE SATELLITE.

They were Englishmen,—London shopkeepers in a small way, I guessed, from their talk. Two of them, father and son, seemed a bit hectoring and dictatorial; the third was an admiring satellite. For very shame's sake

Terence and I didn't like to drop our Dialogue as if we were culprits; so we lowered our voices, and went through it to the bitter end.

Our new companions listened for a moment, and the truculent father said, "Neouw, there y'are, Tom! wot's hall that tork abeout? You kneouw the lingo."

Master Tom—he was about nineteen—posed, apparently, as a linguist. He knew the language all right, he said. "It was kind of debased German. He had picked it up from a boy at school. It was the sime to 'im as Hinglish."

"Wottaw thiy siyin, Tom?" said the father.

"Oh," muttered Tom, "abeout the kaind 'v dai it is, an', hall thet rot. But no use listenin' to them. They tork such a bad patois, an' hungrimmentikil."

The satellite looked impressed. "D'ye tork 't 's wull 's French an' Juh'man?" he asked.

"Hall the sime to me", said Tom. "The sime 'z Hinglish."

The satellite's awe deepened. Presently, however, he spied the cattle in the fields as we sped along. He pointed them out to Tom. "Fine ceouws, miy wu'd!"

THE BACKSLIDER

"Humph! better in Bu'kshire!" replied the linguist.

In a minute or two he broke out again: "Lot 'v ceouws in a field here, Tom!"

"Faugh!" said Tom; "faw mo' 'n Essex!"

But the man of humility had an eye for landscape, and couldn't be repressed.

"Ho, crikkie", he exclaimed, "look at that meadow an' canal. Ain't it stunnin'?"

But the father came to his son's rescue in defence of Old England. "Yeou jist go deouwn Nawf'k wiy! Faw better th'n this wretched 'ole!"

The satellite evidently felt reproved for his lack of patriotism, for he subsided immediately. But he couldn't help himself. You might see by the way he looked out of the window that he was in ecstasies over the glowing panorama before him, in spite of Norfolk and Essex and the contempt of his fellow-travellers.

Meantime Terence, fuming and in disgust, had buried himself in the columns of Tit-Bits. The truculent one recognised the familiar weekly, and drawing his son's attention to both reader and paper he announced quite audibly; "'E can read Hinglish. 'E looks hintelligent."

DO YOU SPEAK ENGLISH?

Advancing half way across the carriage, he cleared his throat, and addressed Terence at the top of his voice.

"Do you—a hem!—a hem!—do you—*speak Hinglish?*"

One could have heard the last two words in the next compartment.

Terence looked up; and I saw by the twinkle in his eye what he was going to do.

"Hein?" he interrogated with a nasal whoop like a subdued trumpet. He had learnt this at school from his French teacher and was a profiscient at rendering it accurately. It gave an unconventional flavour to his manner—which was just what he wished.

"Hein?" he trumpeted again, with an air of amiable curiosity.

"I hawskt—do you—hem!—*speak—Hinglish?*"

"Ze Engels Langwitch? Yes: I shpeak him—von leetle bit. You alzóo?"

"Hi 'm 'n Englishman," said the truculent one proudly, a trifle taken aback.

HE MEANS THE EAST END.

"Zoo?" replied Terence. "Ach zoo. Ja. Jawohl. Zoo gaat 't. Beauti-ful—lang-witch! Beauti—ful!" he enunciated with painful distinctness and many twitches of his face.

All this fell in with the tourists' preconceived ideas of foreign utterance. They exchanged glances.

"You kin mike yors'ff hunderstood, hall raight," interposed the linguist. "Were you ever in London."

"Oh, yes," answered my cousin slowly, counting off upon his fingers. "Alzoo—von—two—tree—time—Mooch peoples—in Londe."

"Did you like London?" queried Truculence Senior.

"Londe?—No! No—boddy like Londe.—Fery ugly! Mooch smoke—alzoo fogk.—Men see nozzing. Mooch poor peoples—No boots."

"Not like London!! Why London's the gritest city in the wu'ld."

"I pity me mooch—for London peoples."

"Let'm aleoun, gov'ner," said the linguist, furious. "It's the Heast End 'e's got in 'is 'ed."

"But the Heouses 'v Pawl'mint—and the Tride?" reasoned the father, reluctant to abandon the controversy.

"Houses Parliament?—nozzing!" said Terence recklessly. "Trade?—alzoo nozzing! American man hef all ze trade. Fery clever. Alzoo German man. Fery clever."

WAKE UP, JOHN BULL.

That was a clincher. Terence had amply avenged their contempt of the scenery they were passing through.

"Let the bloomin' ass aleoun", cried Truculence junior. "'E deoun't kneouw wot 'e's torkin' abeout."

But the shot had gone home. The papers had been full of "Wake up, John Bull!" of late, and he felt uncomfortable. Yet though we relapsed into silence, it wasn't for long. For soon the senior member of the trio got very exasperated with a local railway-guide that he had been consulting. "Bit of a muddle that!" he cried contemptuously, flinging the booklet on the seat. "Cawn't mike 'ed or tile of it!"

He turned to my cousin: "Can you tell me 'ow far it is to Gooday—or Goodee?"

Terence replied briskly in appalling English: "Goodee—I know-not. Zat iss nozzing. Good-day, zat is Goejen-dag!"

"Look 'ere," said the tourist; "'Ere you aw!" pointing to the name of the place on his Cook's ticket.

GOUDA HISTORICAL.

"Oh," said Terence, getting so foreign as to be scarcely intelligible. "Zat-iss—Gouda. Beaut-ti-ful city!" And he rolled his eyes in apparent awe at the magnificence of that unpretentious market-town. "Ex-qui-seet!"

"Ow far is it?" queried his interlocutor. "Ow long, in the trine—to Gouda?"

"Alzoo," returned my cousin, purposely misunderstanding him. "Yes; ferry long. Long times. Ferry old ceety. Much years. Tree—four—century! Historique!"

"Yes, yes," said the impatient traveller. "But—wen—d'we—arrive? get there—you kneouw—?"

"You vil arrivé," pronounced Terence in the same baby-English, "haff—of—ze—klok."

"Hawf 'n eour; that wot 'e's drivin' et," grumbled the Linguist.

They kept on asking questions and criticising us to our faces, when they talked together. Our dress, our appearance, our complexions were all adjudged to be woefully foreign; and they got so patronising that I had to put in an odd word, in real English, to Terence, now and again, just to prevent them going too far. Imperceptibly conversation became general; and as I forced Terence out of his assumed ignorance of English, the surprise of the tourists deepened into dismay, for they noticed we were talking more and more quickly, and idiomatically as well.

FOREIGNERS DON'T GET THE HANG OF IT.

"Hi siy!" whispered the satellite, "they're learnin' Hinglish from hus! I'm blest hif thiy weount soon be nearly 's good 's we are!"

"Never you fear," said young Conceit. "Furriners never git the 'ang of it."

"Never," corroborated Truculence.

But the open criticising of our appearance was at an end.

Our companions looked anything but conciliatory when a crowd of rustics poured into the carriage at one of the stations. It was some sort of market at Gouda; and the bommel was crammed now. Finally the guard scurried along, and half hoisted, half pushed a peasant woman with her three children into the compartment.

It was odd to see Truculence rise and help the little ones in; and odder still to see the children smile up into that formidable face, when they took their seats.

A CONFIDENT YOUNGSTER.

I noticed the twinkle in his eye, however, as he watched the bairnies trying to scramble to the window. He was evidently much interested in a bright little boy of seven with dreamy eyes, who was bent on amusing himself; and I could see that he wanted badly to shake hands with him and his tot of a sister, and ask them their names. He evidently regretted his inability to speak Dutch; but he made up for his silence by reaching the boy the window-strap, with a nod of comradeship. The little fellow took it eagerly and, after playing with it a moment or two, slid off his seat and actually climbed up beside Truculence (the scorner of everything non-British) and pushing Truculence to one side, looked out of Truculence's window.

So surprisingly passive was my severe compatriot at all this that I hazarded a guess, and said: "You have a boy of five at home?"

He stopped short clearing the pane for his tiny companion, and sat stock-still. It might have been a statue that was beside me so little did he move. Not a sound in answer to my question!

Quickly I glanced at him.

Oh, I could have bitten off my tongue when I saw that man's face! It was drawn and white, and not at all like the scornful censor's of a few minutes before.

AN ENGLISH UNCLE FOR CLAAS.

He continued staring out of the window a moment; then he turned and said quietly: "I 'ad—a little fair haired fellow—a year ago..... 'E was six.... An' the born image of thet kiddie there."

Here he stroked the kiddie's head, which was now glued to the glass in an eager endeavour to see a passing train.

"'E used to be that fond of machinery, too," he continued, opening a city bag and bringing out a diminutive flying-machine, a "twee-dekker" that he had evidently bought in the Hague. "I got it, 'cos it minded me of the things my boy used to ply with. But I've nobody to give it to.

May I as well give it to this kid. Tell 'is mother 'e's to keep it. Tell 'er that I'm 's **hold uncle from Hingland**."

I did my best. Claas grasped the situation at once, as far as the twee-dekker was concerned. The mother was slower. Consternation and politeness took away her speech for an instant, but she soon recovered and put Claas through his drill.

"Oh mijnheer, hij is zoo bij de hand!"

DRAM-DRINKING AT EIGHT?

Then she overwhelmed us all with family reminiscences, which none of us understood a word of, but which could not be stopped. It was a relief to get to Gouda; and the tension of our feelings was pleasantly relaxed by observing the profound disgust that mantled the Londoner's brow, when after helping the children on to the platform, he was accosted by a vendor of local dainties, who loudly insisted on selling Goudsche Sprits to the company. "'Ere's a Johnny wants the kiddies an'all of us to liquor up—on neat spirits—before hight o'clock in the mo'nin'! Shime, I call it."

WUIF ES, OOM!

Claas had to say 'Good-bye' to his new uncle, and we watched proceedings from our window. The Linguist ignored the adieu completely; but the Satellite manfully backed up the father, and shook hands all round. A knot of porters gathered to seize the luggage of the big Englishman, who stood, masterful and bored, in the midst of the hubbub. His jaw and chin were those of Rhadamanthus; but his eyes were soft as they rested on the boyish figure descending the stairs with his baby-sister. Claas was waving a small hand to his new uncle who had given him the Twee-dekker; but his new uncle was not waving anything to him. So Claas stopped short, and cried at the top of his voice: "Wuif es oom! wui—uif es, nouw! Je moet wuife!"

"Wot's 'e up to, the young rescal?" he asked me.

"I believe he wants you to make a sign of goodbye. It's always done here," I replied.

Well, he produced, from some place or other, a brilliant jubilee handkerchief—he was a dressy man and had plenty of coloured things—and shook it with both hands to his tiny friend. And the last I saw of him, as the train steamed on towards Utrecht, was, his waving of this silk banner to the little boy on the steps; the stern lips were relaxed into a smile; the defiant face was quite wistful as he repeated: "The young rescal!"

Here the Goudsche sprits seller, in his tour up and down the platform, approached the burly Londoner again, and seeing him now in an unexpectedly melting mood, at once proffered his delicacies with noisy persistence.

"Goudsche sprits! Goudsche sprits! Sir," he bawled in the Englishman's face, holding out a packet.

HIS BARK IS WORSE THAN HIS BITE.

Truculence was quite glad of the interruption. He blew his nose violently on his marvellous handkerchief, and turned upon the local merchant with a glare of indignation.

"Get along! How dare you? D'ye take me for a drunkard?"

"Formidable customer that!" whispered Terence at my elbow. "Still I think his bark is worse than his bite."

"Not a doubt of it," I replied. "And there are more of his kind."

CHAPTER XIII.

BELET!

We got on famously at Utrecht and at the Arnhem station. In less time than it takes to tell it we were mounted on our cycles with our bags in front of us, and ready for the road.

"This is fine!" exclaimed Terence. And indeed it was. Charmed by the ease with which we had got along so safely, I felt a trifle elated over our linguistic victories, and had already begun to dream of fresh fields to conquer, when we drew near van Leeuwen's villa on the Velperweg—a lovely spot.

We dismounted to make sure we were right, and then walked briskly up the avenue.

The door was opened by a timid-looking servant, who said: "Er is belet."

WELKE MIJNHEER?

It was the first time I had met the expression; yet it sounded oddly familiar. Ah, of course. For the last ten days I had been studying *biljetten* out of the railway-guide. There was apparently a slight provincialism in her way of rendering the liquid in the middle of the word, but this didn't matter. **There was a ticket**, then. Puzzling, very.

"Ja?" I said tentatively.

"Er is belet," she repeated. The intonation was decisive; but as her manner was expectant, I took it for a question, had we tickets? Queer, certainly. Yes; I assured her we had,—"gewone biljetten, retour,—geldig voor éen dag."

She shifted her ground and said, "*Mijnheer heeft belet.*"

Now you know how hard it is to be sure what person servants are talking about when they say Mijnheer. Did she mean me or her master? "Welke Mijnheer?" I asked. "Ben ik mijnheer, of is Mijnheer mijnheer?"

Raising her voice she announced deliberately, but with increasing irritation: "*Mijnheer van Leeuwen—heeft—belet.*"

"Aha", I whispered to Terence, "It's my big letter she's talking about. Well, I'm glad it came in time".

AN AANSLAGBILJET.

"Uitstekend!" I hastened to say. "Dat biljet is van mij. Dus mijnheer verwacht mij, niet waar?"

She nervously closed the door a bit. "Ik heb al gezaid—vanmorgen heeft mijnheer *expres belet gegeven*."

"Mag ik het hebben, dan", I enquired politely; "Mijn brief—dat geschreven biljet?"

"Hé?" she said, visibly relieved, opening the door widely as she spoke. "Neem mij niet kwalijk, Mijnheer. Ik wist niet dat u van de belasting was. Komt u om het beschrijvingsbiljet?"

She retreated a step, timidly, into the hall, and glanced at an elderly butler, who in silence had been standing at a discreet distance listening to our colloquy. The butler moved forward, and in an apologetic tone murmured, "Mijnheer, het beschrijvingsbiljet is nog niet klaar. Of komt u met een aanslagbiljet?"

As I had a newspaper in my hand full of talk about a 'moordaanslag' I repudiated the latter idea indignantly. "Geen denken aan!" I said.

The butler came out and stood on the steps, enquiring "Is U soms een schatter."

Schatter? (Schat, a treasure; schatter, a *treasurer*. I reasoned.) "Wel nee: geen schatter ben ik, alleen Eerlijk Secretaris van de Studenten-Club".

A MYSTERIOUS OBSTACLE.

In the hall a loopmeisje and a seamstress stood transfixed with curiosity. How could I get this mad interview terminated?

The deferential butler began to grow suspicious.

"Komt U niet van de belasting?"

"Ik weet het niet," I replied.

That was enough.

"Mijnheer geeft belet altijd 's morgens," he said, adding, evidently with reference to my eerlijk secretaris. "Wij zijn allemaal eerlijk hier!"

We appeared to be dismissed!

"Terence," I said quickly; "Look if b-e-l-e-t is in the dictionary. They always hark back to that."

In a minute he gave a mild shout: "It's here; it means *hindrance*. Ah, I see. Van Leeuwen is hindered seeing us. Hadn't we better go?"

"De belet is niet erg, hoop ik?" I said to the servant; "ik hoop dat Mijnheer spoedig beter zal worden, als het een ziekte is."

Now at last we had mastered the mysteries of belet? No such thing!

WIJ KRIJGEN BELET.

Turning to go, I thought I might as well enquire when van Leeuwen could be seen. "Wanneer kan ik soms Mijnheer zien?" Her reply confounded me: "Vandaag of morgen, maar U moet **b e l e t   v r a g e n**."

Vragen! surely not ask for an obstacle. "U bedoelt **w e i g e r e n**, niet waar?" I suggested.

"Nee: belet vragen, anders zal mijnheer u niet ontvangen."

"Oh Terence!" I exclaimed. "This is too awful! **H e** has this obstacle; he has given it to us; now **w e** must **a s k   i t   a g a i n**. And I don't even know what it is!"

"Take care, Jack. Don't ask anything else, or you'll get us into a worse mess."

"One moment," I said, appealing to the stolid butler. "Moet ik verzoeken om weggestuurd te worden? Of wat?"

"Ja Mijnheer, ik verzoek jullie maar weg te gaan. Alstublieft!"

The solemn man looked like an archbishop. He cleared his throat and added courteously: "Maar, als U Mijnheer van Leeuwen wil spreken, moet U belet **l a t e n   v r a g e n**. Anders **k r i j g t** U belet als U komt."

"Schei uit!" I cried in dismay. "Terence, let us fly! for my brain won't stand it."

IS MIJNHEER GEENGAGEERD?

"No, no!" he interposed hastily. "Don't be silly or hysterical, now. Look here. I've been working the thing out in my head and think I can see some sense in it. Perhaps it's all very simple. Van Leeuwen may be only occupied for the moment, and so can see us if we wait. Just ask if they mean that he's merely engaged. He mayn't be sick at all. There's the word for *engaged*."

And he reached me the dictionary with this thumb opposite: *geengageerd, verpanden, verloofd.*

Yes, I thought. There was wisdom in his calm suggestion, though really I was sick making these curious enquiries. But it seemed plain sailing now. So with an ingratiating smile I just asked in a matter of fact sort of way: "Mijnheer is soms geengageerd? Is het wel?"

"Verloofd?" I added taking the next word, as there was no manner of response forthcoming to the first question.

"Verpanden?" whispered Terence with his eye on the dictionary.

The company—there were some six of them now clustering round the butler for protection—retreated hastily into the recesses of the big hall, and left that majestic man to shut the door. This he did without delay, saying, somewhat nervously, "Maak dat jullie weg gaat!"

EEN SPOEDIGE RESTAURATIE.

There was nothing left for us to do but to beat a dignified retreat.

I made it as dignified as possible by, expressing our best wishes for van Leeuwen's speedy recovery.

"Komplimenten aan Mijnheer, hoor; een spoedige restauratie!"

We cycled off.

CHAPTER XIV.

THE DAY-TRAIN.

We had a delightful spin along the Velperweg.

Dismounting three or four times to admire choice 'bits' of scenery, we were enticed on and on, and followed a side way that rose over a gentle slope. From the ridge of this acclivity we could watch the cloud shadows, violet and purple, sweeping over wide moors, and by their subtle contrasts bringing out the soft shimmering of the distant sunlight. On the horizon we made out the river and some hill-tops marked on our maps. Terence was confident he saw Nijmegen; but pushing on to get a still finer view, we came to grief in crossing a heather "brae". At least I did. The front wheel was wrenched to one side; and we had to foot it all the way to Velp. There having left both machines at a cycle-mender's, we started for a long tramp.

LOST IN THE WOOD.

That was a grand mistake, for we went too far. There were other ranges of wooded hills to be climbed, and the air was exhilarating. The time passed quickly, so it was late in the afternoon before we knew. Feeling more or less famished, we ventured on a short cut through the "Onzalige Bosch"; but soon were hopelessly lost. It **w a s** a task to get on the main road.

Indeed we took several wrong turnings apparently, for they seemed—it was hard to get our proper orientation—to bring us back to the same neighbourhood always. But at last we came to a line of wooded hills, and discovered a cart track that led us to a real high-way. This high-way was a magnificent affair with high over-arching trees; and on it, to our great relief, there were tram-rails!

STOPT DE TRAM OP EEN WENK?

Help was near at hand. We put our best foot foremost, so to speak, and hurried forward looking in the dusk for a *halte*. Perhaps we may have passed some *halten*, but we didn't notice any; and as we were fagged out, I was glad to come upon a group of workmen who, I imagined, could tell me about the tram. The question I wanted to get solved was simple. Did the tram stop merely at the official *halten*, or would the driver pull up anywhere he got a passenger? If the bye-laws of this particular tramway allowed the tram to stop and pick up pedestrians anywhere all along the line, we were quite safe; we should just sit down on the roadside and rest. We shouldn't walk another step.

The men were shovelling away at fallen leaves, so I accosted them in my friendliest Dutch and said: "Stop de tram overal?" As this was greeted with the customary "*blief?*" I tried to be more explicit. "Stop de tram op een wenk of een uitroepteeken? Of stopt hij alleen op de halten?"

This puzzled them all exceedingly; and one elderly man mopped his brow with his handkerchief and said, "Ik mot es eve prakiseere."

PRAKISEERE.

With that he stabbed his spade into the sod at his foot and leaned on the top of it with both arms, his eye fixed the while on me. I didn't care for the performance, as his stare was discomfitingly steady; but I allowed him for a while to prakiseere undisturbed.

Indeed I couldn't even guess what he was trying to do. It looked like an exercise in philosophic meditation or an attempt to hypnotise me on the spot, and as he seemed in no hurry to give me the information I desired, there was nothing for it but ask one of the other road menders.

Selecting the most intelligent looking of them. I said "Kijk es, baas; houdt de tram op, op een wuiving van een zakdoek? Of als men teekent met een paraplu?"

This second functionary shook his head sadly, and leaned on *his* spade in turn, gazing at me as if I had horns. There was a third man—close at hand—quite a young fellow, halfway across the road where he was standing as if petrified by my previous conversation. However he wasn't "prakiseering," so I stepped across to him with the slowly enunciated query: "Vertel me nou es: wat voor signaal moet ik maken, als ik wensch op genomen te worden?"

He was the promptest of the group, for he replied glibly: "Ik weet het niet. Je mot eve by de Politie gaan vragen." But not a word about the tram.

MY DUTCH BREAKS DOWN.

I gave it up. No information could possibly be extracted from these roadmen. My Dutch had quite broken down, and in disgust, I surrendered the leading of the expedition wholly to Terence.

Terence has a theory that he can make his meaning clear by means of careful and scientific gesticulation. Now he took his innings, while I watched the proceedings from a comfortable seat by the roadside.

"They're quite clever at it," he shouted to me. "The tram will be here in two somethings—I believe two hours—so we may as well move on: it'll be no use to us, to wait."

"All right," I said; "your way of it!" And off we started, tired as we were. We weren't ten minutes on the road till the tram was heard puffing behind us; and catching sight of a kind of double line in front of us we bounded towards this spot in hopes there might be a halte there. There *was*: and the tram waited half an hour at it, and then went back again the way it had come. We had to walk. Well, at all events we reached Velp at dark. My cycle was nicely mended, so after getting some refreshments in an excellent *logement* and taking a prolonged and well earned rest, we mounted our bikes and rode straight to Arnhem.

THE TRAIN THAT NEVER STOPS.

So disgusted was I with my ill-success in Dutch that I tackled the porters in English. An obliging w i t - j a s asked me if I would have the day-train. "Rather not," I told him. "There will surely be another train to-night. It's only nine."

The first was a bommel, he said, and would do for the fietsen; but he recommended us to wait for the day-train.

"What! And stay here all night?" I asked.

"No," he explained. "Day-trein will be here soon."

"**H o w i s t h a t ?**" said I. "**H o w** in the wide world can a **D a y - t r a i n g o a t n i g h t**? or is it because it started from Germany by day-light? You surely don't reckon here by Amerikaansche tijd for the sake of the tourists?"

"You not understand," he explained. "We call it day-trein becos' you pay more—."

"Well!" I interrupted; "that would be a Pay-train, then! Not Day."

"No, no," he said excitedly. "Zis trein go kwik!—not stop—**a n y w h e r e s**!"

"But if it doesn't stop, how can we get in?" I asked. "Of moet ik **b e l e t v r a g e n** voor deze Dag-trein? Geeft de trein belet? You'll need a special kind of ticket, too—perhaps an aanslagsbiljet?"

"No, no; only little bewijsje—kwik trein—bring Restoration—becos'—."

"What? The Restoration! It turns day into night, and brings back Charles II! Go on, please, I can believe anything now!"

MET HANGENDE POOTJES—RE INFECTA.

"Hallo! is this where you are?" sounded gratefully on our ears. It was van Leeuwen, who had been expecting us all day, after he had heard about our call, from the indignant butler. He had given up all hope of seeing us, but we passed him by in the dark, talking and laughing. He had followed hot-speed to the station—in time to explain the mysteries of the D-trein. My spirits rose. The world was still ruled by reason. Of course we went back with our rescuer. That was the original plan, and I had a grammar to send with him to the Hague.

As he waited, talking to Terence, I recalled the cycles. The wit-jas demurred: "De fietsen zijn al weg."

"Neen, niet waar," I told him. "Onmogelijk, hoor! Geen trein is weg. Daar zijn de papiertjes ervan. Pak ze: breng de fietsen mee. Ik weiger je verontschuldigingen. Doe wat ik zeg, ik bid U. En niet terug komen met hangende pootjes!"

CHAPTER XV.

SUPPER AT A BOERDERIJ.

That night, after Terence had retired, I had a confidential talk with van Leeuwen; and I begged of him, as a great favour, to take the Grammar to Kathleen, and—if he had time—give her a little coaching in Dutch. He said he would—to oblige me; and I was pleased to notice that he started, taking Boyton with him, by the earliest possible train. This was the six twenty—a notorious bommel which brought him into the Hague only seventeen minutes earlier than if he had waited for a decent breakfast.

Enderby got to Arnhem about noon, and took us 'in tow' for our cycling tour. We had a glorious week of it in Gelderland under his direction; but there were no adventures worth speaking of. In ten days we were back at the Residentie, as 'brown as berries and as gay as larks'. It is Terence's phrase, and I give it for what it's worth.

But at all events van Leeuwen was gay enough now. His pedagogic labours seemed to suit him, and Kathleen was quite herself again. To hear her laugh now was to imagine that you were back in Kilkenny in the days before the suffragette question was mooted.

IN THE SHADE OF THE PRIEELTJE.

We were all delighted. Except perhaps Enderby. That youth didn't appear more than half pleased at the turn things had taken; but he had the grace to keep out of the way and consoled himself with motoring. One day—I had only sat down to luncheon—he carried me off for a great run to the islands south of Rotterdam. But the machine broke down twice before we reached Dordrecht, and we had to content ourselves with housing its fragments in a shed, and walking to a *boerderij* where my friend was well known. Here, indeed, we were expected to supper; but we arrived hours before we were due, and *minus* an automobile. This necessitated explanations, which Enderby seemed gracefully enough to make to the family party in the garden. In a shady p r i e e l t j e there, they regaled us with "liemonade"; and I occasioned some consternation by rising twice to offer my seat to the mother and daughter respectively, who came in after I had sat down. They wouldn't take the chair I vacated for them, and appeared to resent my civility. Enderby, too, made me uncomfortable by touching my foot and saying, *sotto voce*, "Take care what you're about, O'Neill".

Baas Willemse was very sympathetic about the mishap to our motor, and strongly recommended the services of a gifted blacksmith of his acquaintance.

Indeed, before we knew, he had a pony harnessed in a sort of hooded tax-cart, in which he insisted in driving Enderby to this wonderful mechanic, to have the damaged car put to rights. And off they started.

AN UNPREPARED GUEST.

It was only then that I realized the situation. Here was I—without dictionary or phrase-book—left to play the part of intelligent guest, unaided and unprepared. And that was the first time in my life I was 'spending the evening' in a non-English-speaking home. How would I get through it? I did hope that the local Vulcan would be quick.

At first it wasn't so bad. What with remarks about "het prachtige weer" and "het ongeluk", and what with playing with the children, I got along quite smoothly for a while.

I even discoursed a little about the beauty of the afternoon-sunlight and "het schilderachtige van het zomerlandschap".

COWS' OVERCOATS.

All this was taken in such good part that I went further afield; and noticing a large number of cattle with odd coverings on their backs, I ventured on a comparison which I fancied might interest the company. "In Groot-Brittanje hebben de koeien niet zoo dikwijls overjassen. Mag ik beleefd vragen: gebeurt dat hier van wege de gezelligheid, of van wege de gezondheid, of voor het mooi?"

They were all pleased at this, and gave me a lot of talk about cows—which didn't make me much the wiser.

By violent efforts I recalled some of my old choice phrases, and passed myself somehow. But alas! supper came; and then my real troubles began.

We all adjourned to a binnen-kamer, where an ample spread awaited us. I was given the seat of honour. It was a great pity, all agreed, that Mijnheer Enderby wasn't back: but they thought I might be hungry. Well, I was—and with reason. Nothing to eat since breakfast!

"Thee of chocolaat, Mijnheer?"

"Thee, alstublieft", I said.—And I got it.

"Krentebroodjes?"

THANK YOU.

"Dank U," I answered pleasantly, and reached for one in a leisurely manner. You don't like to parade your hunger, you know. Well, I hadn't been prompt enough. A plateful from which I was about to help myself, was removed. The action surprised me, and I looked for a moment at the mother, who had withdrawn the dainties so unexpectedly. She looked at me, slightly ruffled. But no krentebroodjes!

"Wil mijnheer een broodje met vleesch?"

"Oh dank U wel," I said, endeavouring to be quicker. That time I nearly had a slice. But the agile youth, Jaap, who was in charge of the plate, whipped it away too.

No broodjes met vleesch for me! It was very queer.

"Soms een ei?" said the dignified grandmother, in a white cap with gold ornaments. She presided, and did a great deal of the talking; and I could make out that she was the widow of a fisherman or shipowner in a small way, and had once visited Hull. In virtue of having spent a week there, some forty years before, she was regarded evidently by all the rest as an authority on English manners and customs and language and literature.

"Soms een ei?" she pleaded. "Engelshman like egg."

Very much, indeed, I thought, if I could only get one—call me English or Irish or whatever you like. Fain would I have had an egg off that plate, where she had just put down six or eight, freshly boiled.

Determined to get one, if politeness would assist me, I smiled and bowed and smiled again. "Oh, ik dank U duizendmaal. Ik bewijs volkomen dankbaarheid."

ANOTHER CUP.

Stunned apparently by my reply, she hesitated. To encourage her to extend these edibles a trifle nearer, I said, "Alstublieft. Dank U." But she only sighed, and laid the plate out of reach, reproachfully.

No eggs!

"Truitje," she whispered to her granddaughter; "presenteer de schuimpjes."

Truitje didn't say a word, but pushed a schaaltje of these light refreshments towards me.

I did secure two; but in a moment they were finished. You see, a schuimpje doesn't last very long, when you are really hungry.

Then the mother complained, courteously, of my slender appetite: "Mijnheer wil niets gebruiken."

"O ja," I interrupted, "integendeel! Heel graag. Alstublieft." And to show I meant it, I asked for another cup of tea. "Mag ik beleefdelijk vragen om een andere kop?" Here I reached cup and saucer towards them.

VOOR DE PRONK.

That certainly created a diversion. They looked blankly at one another, till the grandmother—she was very hearty—called out with a cheerful laugh, "Hé, ja. Dat's waar ook. De Engelsche koppen zijn groot."

"Truitje," she whispered in an audible aside. "Breng even een Engelsche kom. Ze staan in de kast."

"Zie zoo. Mijnheer," she continued to me with a pleasant smile. "Nouw, Mijnheer wil zeker nog wat thee hebben? Nouw, niet bedanken, hoor."

"Oh ja," I replied joyfully, "Schiet op—Als'tublieft—dank U. Dank U—heelemaal!"

Holding the tea-pot poised in her hand, she looked at me appealingly, but in doubt. "Wat? heus?" she said.

What was I to do?

I looked at her quite as appealingly, and replied. "Ja, heus! Wel zeker."

That was decisive. No tea!

The cup, however, was planted down in front of me, upside down. "Het is voor de pronk, zeker," said the grandmother. "Engelsche gewoonte—zeer net."

But conversation flagged. The silence was painful. You could have heard a pin drop. My discreet attempt to ask for something had failed, and I didn't see exactly how I was to improve upon it.

THINGS ARE DEAR IN HOLLAND.

The mother meantime surveyed my empty plate and empty cup with distinct disapproval, and put out a feeler: "Mijnheer houdt niet van Hollandsche kost?"

'Hollandsch kost', what things **c o s t** in Holland—Dutch prices, in other words? Well, they are rather high sometimes. The remark seemed somewhat irrelevant, but it was talk, and therefore welcome. Anything to break that oppressive silence. Eagerly embracing the opportunity of saying something, I responded with cordiality: "Hollandsche kost? Neen. Ik houd niet erg ervan. Dat kan U begrijpen. Ze zijn veels te hoog!"

This well-meant pleasantry was received with such evident disfavour that I hastened to explain. "Ik bedoel dat vele artikelen zijn kostbaar—of kostelijk—mijns bedunkens—in Holland—maar van onberispelijke smaak."

Hardly any response was made to this.—The merest murmur on the part of the grandmother, that was all. But they all looked at me curiously, without saying a word.

Frantically I strove to make an observation in an easy friendly way, but all my Dutch seemed to have deserted me.—At least all I judged suitable.

Fragments of conversation did float through my agonized brain, but none of them was quite what I needed.

"Ik graauw, ik kef en kweel" was out of the question.

AN INNOCENT OBSERVATION.

Two proverbs suddenly flashed across my mind, and I gripped them firmly. One was: "Een vogel in de hand is meer waard dan tien in de lucht," and the tempting parallel offered itself: "Eén broodje in de hand is meer waard dan tien op een bord." As this aphorism, however, didn't sound extra civil, I let it pass.

"Deugd en belooning gaan zelden te samen" was the second proverb; and on that model I managed, after due cogitation, to construct a nice harmless phrase. As it expressed what we all knew and could see before our eyes, I felt safe against contradiction, and I knew it couldn't hurt anybody. This dictum ran: "Koek en boterham gaan dikwijls te samen."

Perhaps it was owing to the suddenness with which I proclaimed this truth, or to some severity in my manner; but the effect produced on the company was magical.

Jaap dropped his fork with a clatter and said, "Gunst!" The mother put her hand to her chest, whispering. "Zoo'n schrik!" All looked startled and stopped eating!

HALF-ELF.

To divert the scrutiny of so many eyes, I manufactured talk on the first thing that occurred to me, and, reverting to the Dutch prices, said: "Sommige artikelen in Holland zijn duur. Van morgen heb ik een plaat bezichtigd—een poes opgerold over een kannetje melk—de zee in de verte. Prachtig. Maar peper-duur. Tien gulden en een half."

"Wat zegt mijnheer," asked the grandmother, "van de poes en de peper en de tien gulden?"

Assuring her it was merely a 'plaat', but one that was 'erg kostbaar', I grasped at the analogy of the hours of the day, to do full justice to the expensiveness of the picture. If ten o'clock and a half works out at "half-elf-uur," it is not hard to reckon what ten guilders-and-a-half *ought* to be; so I gave it with relish: "En, Juffrouw, wat denkt U? Het kost half-elf-gulden!"

Jaap looked at his watch and shook his head. Then he shook the watch, put it back in his pocket and fastened his eyes again on me.

"Nee, hoor!" exclaimed the mother, who had now begun to help a special dish; "Nee; zoo laat is het niet. Mijnheer O'Neill, neem een stukje pudding—toe dan—heel verteerbaar."

STARVATION IN THE MIDST OF PLENTY.

My plate was passed along, and was heaped up liberally. Though I waited with my thanks as long as I could, I was obliged to intervene when the plate was piled high enough for any two people. "Nouw, ik bedank!" I ejaculated, making my best bow.

But that caused the guillotine to fall once more. With a gesture of impatience Truitje put away my verteerbaar pudding on a remote side-table. Not the least chance of getting it!

I was starving in the midst of plenty!

As my hosts appeared to be as much impressed with the contrast as I was, I endeavoured to smooth things over a little, and set them more at their ease. Making the best of it, with all the careless grace I could muster I blandly assured them that it didn't matter. "Het geeft niets—het hindert niet—het komt er niet opaan."

But they grew huffy and distant—my phrases didn't do much to relieve the strain—and I was feeling more depressed and famished every minute, when, to my unspeakable relief, up there came the sound of wheels on the gravel, and in a moment I heard Enderby's voice talking Dutch loudly and confidently in the hall.

A MOHAMMEDAN.

The young folks all rushed out to meet him (he is a prime favourite with them) and there was much whispering and laughing and a long confabulation before they came back.

Enderby entered, and greeted the older people merrily: but there was a quizzical frown upon his brow as he sat down near me. "What's all this O'Neill?" he whispered. "Are you ill?"

"I'm as well as could be expected in the circumstances."

"Circumstances! Why you wouldn't touch the good food they gave you. Not content with despising their cookery you objected to their tea-cups, and pretend that religious scruples keep you from eating until after half-past ten. They think you are some kind of Mohammedan. These kind people are a little hurt, I fear; and I can see they are greatly astonished."

"So am I! I have been as polite as anything, all the time; but though they offer me plenty of everything, if I attempt to help myself, whew!—they whisk the dish away. They may be hurt, as you say; but I can tell you, *I'm starving.* Is there no way to——."

Our conversation was interrupted by the mother's voice, which broke in with the cheery question: "Mijnheer Enderby houdt **w e l** van Hollandsche kost, niet waar?"

PROBEER NOUW IS.

I watched what he would say.

He used two easy words: "Dat spreekt."

Busying herself with plates and spoons, the mother continued: "U neemt een beetje avondeten?"

"Nouw! Of ik!" said Enderby with enthusiasm—and they brought him eatables all sorts.

These dainties caught my eye in spite of myself; and I wondered why none had been given to me. It was now going on to ten; and I had had nothing since early breakfast, except a glass of lemonade, a cup of tea and two small schuimpjes.

The old lady was observant, and must have detected famine in my eye, for with a glance at the clock she called softly to Truitje: "Probeer nouw is."

To me she said, "Wil Mijnheer nog thee?"

The secret was mine now, and I didn't hesitate.

"Of ik!" I replied.

OPEN SESAME.

There was a scream of delight from all quarters! My kom was turned right-side up and filled to the brim with fresh warm tea. I was the centre of interest at once. Cupboards flew open on all sides, like pistol-shots, and everybody was waiting to help me. It was who would give me most.

"Ham en een broodje?"

"Of ik!"

"Rookvleesch—en een ei?"

"Of ik!"

The seven lean years were past, now the time of plenty was come.

"Bitterkoekjes en leverworst?"—"Muisjes en karnemelk?"—"Appelbolletjes, wentelteefjes en molsla?"—I refused nothing.

"Of ik" was the "Open Sesame"—the key to unlock all cupboards and all hearts.

I took care to thank nobody for anything, for fear my plate would be removed. Happy laughter was heard on all sides. Smiles beamed on every face. In an instant I had become the most popular man on the island,—at all events with the people in that farm-house. Their hospitality and my hunger had met at last, and come to terms—to the unbounded enthusiasm of all.

Meantime Enderby had communicated to them the fact that I was an Irishman; and I overheard someone venture on the singular criticism: "De Ieren zijn zoo lief voor elkaar! Hij gebruikt niets als zijn vriend er niet bij is."

"Hé, wat lief!" said Baas Willemse.

"Innig!" whispered the grandmother, smiling.

"Leuk", answered the mother.

"Aardig", said some one else.

"Typisch", exclaimed Truitje.

A grumble fell on our ears: "Wat gek!"

It was Jaap.

AN AFFECTIONATE IRISH TERRIER.

Truitje talked on one side of Enderby; Jaap talked on the other. Enderby smiled, then sniggered, then laughed; and finally, laying down his knife and fork, he looked at me, and leaned back in his chair and positively roared.

"Well, what's the matter?" I asked austerely.

"She says it's touching to see your affection for me. You looked so melancholy when I was away, as if you were longing for something—or crossed in love—or disappointed! You've won their hearts, at last, my boy, not a doubt of it. Still, don't overdo that phrase, now that you've got it. Jaap here has a story about an Irish terrier in Drenthe that refused to eat anything for three days, when its master was away in Amsterdam. But he adds that the terrier made up for it, by eating everything it could, when its master came back. I can see that you are going to achieve a reputation that will outrival that of your canine compatriot, unless you have a care. Be a bit cautious, please."

GENERAL PRINCIPLES.

Here Jaap, dimly apprehending that Enderby was speaking about him, performed a mystic rite that puzzled me extremely.

Pretending to sharpen an imaginary pencil on his forefinger he held it towards us and cried, "Sliep uit."

"What on earth is that?" I asked Enderby—who, however, could only tell me that it was intended as a roguish taunt—Jaap was always a schelm—but the phrase was otherwise meaningless.

As such I jotted it down at once in my notebook for future use.

From these experiences in the boerderij I was able to deduce an important general principle of practical value.

If you want anything in Holland never say "thank you", until the object is firmly in your grasp. Then you may be as civil as you like. But before you get hold of it, you are only safe if you say, "If I".

In the Dutch language premature thanks are equivalent to a refusal; so you'd better keep your gratitude out of sight.

Well, I had won all hearts here in virtue of my discoveries. As we were going away the grandmother gave me a second Good-bye, shaking me warmly by both hands. "Heeft mijnheer zich goed geamuseerd?" she enquired.

A PARTING SALVO.

"Kostelijk—Uitstekend—Nouw!" was my prompt reply, for I had expected that query.

"Wat spreekt mijnheer nouw makkelijk Hollandsch!" she exclaimed.

"Gunst, ja", was my retort. "Ik heb zoo'n pret gehad! Onbetaalbaar!"

But I caught Jaap's eye; it was critical; so to pay back the youth for his terrier-story I took out my pencil, sharpened it in full view of them all and said, "Sliep uit, Jaap; je bent een schelm".

With that they all cheered, young and old, saying "Net, Mijnheer, net!"

"Tot weerziens!" laughed the grandmother shaking hands again. "Kom spoedig terug".

"Ja hoor; dat spreekt."

"Belooft u?" she repeated, before she let me go.

I pulled myself together, and gave a parting salvo: "Ja, zeker—Stellig—Och kom!—Reken er op!—Of ik!!"

We drove away in a perfect tornado of applause.

EPILOGUE.

On reaching my rooms at Ferdinand Bolstraat 66*a*, the landlady greeted me with respectful effusion and told me that Jan was as good as cured, though the wounded arm would remain stiff for a good while, she feared. She was loud in the praises of the Engelsche juffrouw and her profisciency in Dutch; and (sinking her voice confidentially) Mijnheer van Leeuwen had left a letter for me upstairs.

"Boyton", I thought, as I climbed those forty nine precipitous steps that led to my room, "I hope you have done your duty."

And he had.

THE EXPECTED SURPRISE.

Van Leeuwen wrote that he would prepare me for a great surprise! It was yet a profound secret; but,—well, in fact—that is to say—he was engaged to my cousin Kathleen. They had discovered mutual sympathies and affinities over the study of Dutch—to which language now my cousin was devoting her serious attention. By the by they had been delighted with that monograph of mine. And the queer Grammar was useful. (I should think so!)

He said that he could well imagine my astonished looks when I got this news about his attachment! Now confess, he concluded, that you hadn't the ghost of a suspicion as to what was coming?

"Oh hadn't I just?" I soliloquized, "Well; there's only one thing, my dear fellow, to say to all that; And I really must say it in Dutch: O f   i k ?"

Lightning Source UK Ltd.
Milton Keynes UK
UKHW041611100822
407118UK00003B/849